Introduction to Deep Learning

Eugene Charniak

The MIT Press
Cambridge, Massachusetts
London, England

This book was set in LATEX by author. Printed and bound in the United States of America.

Library of Congress Cataloging-in-Publication Data is available.
ISBN: 978-0-262-03951-2

10   9   8   7   6   5   4   3   2   1

To my family, once more

Contents

Preface

Your author is a long-time artificial-intelligence researcher whose field of expertise, natural-language processing, has been revolutionized by deep learning. Unfortunately, it took him (me) a long time to catch on to this fact. I can rationalize this since this is the third time neural networks have threatened a revolution but only the first time they have delivered. Nevertheless, I suddenly found myself way behind the times and struggling to catch up. So I did what any self-respecting professor would do, scheduled myself to teach the stuff, started a crash course by surfing the web, and got my students to teach it to me. (This last is not a joke. In particular, the head undergraduate teaching assistant for the course, Siddarth (Sidd) Karramcheti, deserves special mention.)

This explains several prominent features of this book. First, it is short. I am a slow learner. Second, it is very much project driven. Many texts, particularly in computer science, have a constant tension between topic organization and organizing material around specific projects. Splitting the difference is often a good idea, but I find I learn computer science material best by sitting down and writing programs, so my book largely reflects my learning habits. It was the most convenient way to put it down, and I am hoping many in the expected audience will find it helpful as well.

Which brings up the question of the expected audience. While I hope many CS practitioners will find this book useful for the same reason I wrote it, as a teacher my first loyalty is to my students, so this book is primarily intended as a textbook for a course on deep learning. The course I teach at Brown is for both graduate and undergraduates and covers all the material herein, plus some "culture" lectures (for graduate credit a student must add a significant final project). Both linear algebra and multivariate calculus are required. While the actual quantity of linear-algebra material is not that great, students have told me that without it they would have found thinking about multilevel networks, and the tensors they require, quite difficult. Multivariate calculus, however, was a much closer call. It appears explicitly only in Chapter 1, when we build up to back-propagation from scratch and I would not be surprised if an extra lecture on partial derivatives would do. Last, there is a probability and statistics prerequisite. This simplifies the exposition and I certainly want to encourage students to take such a course. I also assume a rudimentary knowledge of programming in Python. I do not include this in the text, but my course has an extra "lab" on basic Python.

That your author was playing catch-up when writing this book also explains the fact that in almost every chapter's section on further reading you will find, beyond the usual references to important research papers, many reference to secondary sources — others' educational writings. I would never have learned this material without them.

Providence, Rhode Island
January 2018

Chapter 1

Feed-Forward Neural Nets

It is standard to start exploring *deep learning* (or *neural nets* — we use the terms interchangeably) with their use in computer vision. This area of artificial intelligence has been revolutionized by the technique and its basic starting point — *light intensity* — is represented naturally by real numbers, which are what neural nets manipulate.

To make this more concrete, consider the problem of identifying hand-written digits — the numbers from zero to nine. If we were to start from scratch, we would first need to build a camera to focus light rays in order to build up an image of what we see. We would then need light sensors to turn the light rays into electrical impulses that a computer can "sense." And finally, since we are dealing with digital computers, we would need to *discretize* the image — that is, represent the colors and intensities of the light as numbers in a two-dimensional array. Fortunately, we have a dataset on line in which all this has been done for us — the *Mnist* dataset (pronounced "em-nist"). (The "nist" here comes from the U.S. *National Institute of Standards* (or *nist*), which was responsible for gathering the data.) In this data each image is a 28 * 28 array of integers as in Figure 1.1. (I have removed the left and right border regions to make it fit better on the page.)

In Figure 1.1, 0 can be thought of as white, 255 as black, and numbers in between as shades of gray. We call these numbers *pixel values*, where a *pixel* is the smallest portion of an image that our computer can resolve. The actual "size" of the area in the world represented by a pixel depends on our camera, how far away it is from the object surface, etc. But for our simple digit problem we need not worry about this. The black and white image is show in Figure 1.2.

Looking at this image closely can suggest some simpleminded ways we

1

	7	8	9	10	11	12	13	14	15	16	17	18	19	20
0	0	0	0	0	0	0	0	0	0	0	0	0	0	0
1	0	0	0	0	0	0	0	0	0	0	0	0	0	0
2	0	0	0	0	0	0	0	0	0	0	0	0	0	0
3	0	0	0	0	0	0	0	0	0	0	0	0	0	0
4	0	0	0	0	0	0	0	0	0	0	0	0	0	0
5	0	0	0	0	0	0	0	0	0	0	0	0	0	0
6	0	0	0	0	0	0	0	0	0	0	0	0	0	0
7	185	159	151	60	36	0	0	0	0	0	0	0	0	0
8	254	254	254	254	241	198	198	198	198	198	198	198	198	170
9	114	72	114	163	227	254	225	254	254	254	250	229	254	254
10	0	0	0	0	17	66	14	67	67	67	59	21	236	254
11	0	0	0	0	0	0	0	0	0	0	0	83	253	209
12	0	0	0	0	0	0	0	0	0	0	22	233	255	83
13	0	0	0	0	0	0	0	0	0	0	129	254	238	44
14	0	0	0	0	0	0	0	0	0	59	249	254	62	0
15	0	0	0	0	0	0	0	0	0	133	254	187	5	0
16	0	0	0	0	0	0	0	0	9	205	248	58	0	0
17	0	0	0	0	0	0	0	0	126	254	182	0	0	0
18	0	0	0	0	0	0	0	75	251	240	57	0	0	0
19	0	0	0	0	0	0	19	221	254	166	0	0	0	0
20	0	0	0	0	0	3	203	254	219	35	0	0	0	0
21	0	0	0	0	0	38	254	254	77	0	0	0	0	0
22	0	0	0	0	31	224	254	115	1	0	0	0	0	0
23	0	0	0	0	133	254	254	52	0	0	0	0	0	0
24	0	0	0	61	242	254	254	52	0	0	0	0	0	0
25	0	0	0	121	254	254	219	40	0	0	0	0	0	0
26	0	0	0	121	254	207	18	0	0	0	0	0	0	0
27	0	0	0	0	0	0	0	0	0	0	0	0	0	0

Figure 1.1: An Mnist discretized version of an image

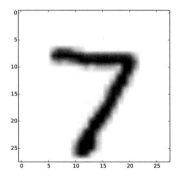

Figure 1.2: A black on white image from the pixels of Figure 1.1

might go about our task. For example, notice that the pixel in position $[8, 8]$ is dark. Given that this is an image of a '7' this is quite reasonable. Similarly, 7s often have a light patch in the middle — i.e., pixel $[13, 13]$ has a zero as its intensity value. Contrast this with the number '1', which often has the opposite values for these two positions since a standard drawing of the number does not occupy the upper left-hand corner but does fill the exact middle. With a little thought we could come up with a lot of *heuristics* (rules that often work, but may not always) such as those, and then write a classification program using them.

However, this is not what we are going to do, since in this book we concentrate on *machine learning*. That is, we approach tasks by asking how we can enable a computer to learn by giving it examples along with the correct answer. In this case we want our program to learn how to identify 28*28 images of digits by giving examples of them along with the answers (also called *labels*). In machine learning we would say that this is a *supervised learning* problem or, to be more emphatic, a *fully supervised learning* problem, in that for every learning example we also give the computer the correct answer. In later chapters, e.g., Chapter 6, we do not have this luxury. There we have a *semi-supervised* problem, or even, in Chapter 7, *unsupervised learning*. We see in those chapters how this can work.

Once we have abstracted away the details of dealing with the world of light rays and surfaces, we are left with a *classification problem* — given a set of inputs (often called *features*), identify (or *classify*) the entity which gave rise to those inputs (or has those features) as one of a finite number of alternatives. In our case the inputs are pixels, and the classification is into ten possibilities. We denote the vector of l inputs (pixels) as $\mathbf{x} = [x_1, x_2 \ldots x_l]$ and the answer is a. In general the inputs are real numbers and may be both positive and negative, though in our case they are all positive integers.

1.1 Perceptrons

We start, however, with a simpler problem. We create a program to decide if an image is a zero or not a zero. This is a *binary classification problem*. One of the earliest machine learning schemes for binary classification is the *perceptron*, shown in Figure 1.3.

Perceptrons were invented as simple computational models of neurons. A single neuron (see Figure 1.4) typically has many inputs (*dendrites*), a *cell body*, and a single output (the *axon*). Echoing this, the perceptron takes

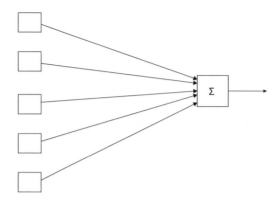

Figure 1.3: Schematic diagram of a perceptron

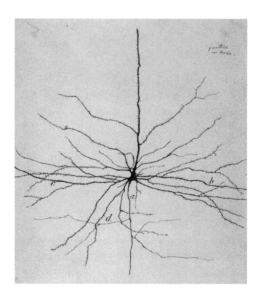

Figure 1.4: A typical neuron

many inputs and has one output. A simple perceptron for deciding if our $28 * 28$ image is of a zero would have 784 inputs, one for each pixel, and one output. For ease in drawing, the perceptron in Figure 1.3 has five inputs.

A perceptron consists of a vector of *weights* $\mathbf{w} = [w_1 \dots w_m]$, one for each input, plus a distinguished weight b, called the *bias*. We call $\mathbf{w}$ and b the *parameters* of the perceptron. More generally, we use Φ to denote parameters, with $\phi_i \in \Phi$ the ith parameter. For a perceptron $\Phi = \{\mathbf{w} \cup b\}$.

With these parameters the perceptron computes the following function:

$$f_\Phi(\mathbf{x}) = \begin{cases} 1 & \text{if } b + \sum_{i=1}^{l} x_i w_i > 0 \\ 0 & \text{otherwise} \end{cases} \tag{1.1}$$

Or in words, we multiply each perceptron input by the weight for that input and add the bias. If this value is greater than zero we return 1, otherwise 0. Perceptrons, remember, are binary classifiers, so 1 indicates that $\mathbf{x}$ is a member of the class and 0, not a member.

It is standard to define the *dot product* of two vectors of length l as

$$\mathbf{x} \cdot \mathbf{y} = \sum_{i=1}^{l} x_i y_i \tag{1.2}$$

so we can simplify the notation for the perceptron computation as follows:

$$f_\Phi(\mathbf{x}) = \begin{cases} 1 & \text{if } b + \mathbf{w} \cdot \mathbf{x} > 0 \\ 0 & \text{otherwise} \end{cases} \tag{1.3}$$

Elements that compute $b + \mathbf{w} \cdot \mathbf{x}$ are called *linear units* and as in Figure 1.3 we identify them with a Σ. Also, when we discuss adjusting the parameters it is useful to recast the bias as another weight in $\mathbf{w}$, one whose feature value is always 1. (This way we only need to talk about adjusting the $\mathbf{w}$s.)

We care about perceptrons because there is a remarkably simple and robust algorithm — the *perceptron algorithm* — for finding these Φ given *training examples*. We indicate which example we are discussing with a superscript, so the input for the kth example is $\mathbf{x}^k = [x_1^k \dots x_l^k]$ and its answer is a^k. For a binary classifier such as a perceptron, the answer is a 1 or 0 indicating membership in the class, or not. When classifying into m classes, the answer would be an integer from 0 to $m - 1$.

It is sometimes useful to characterize machine learning as a *function approximation* problem. From this point of view a single unit perceptron defines a *parameterized class* of functions. Learning the perceptron weights is then picking out the member of the class that best approximates the solution function — the "true" function that, given any set of pixel values, correctly characterizes the image as, say, a zero or not.

As in all machine-learning research, we assume we have at least two and preferably three sets of problem examples. The first is the *training set*. It is used to adjust the parameters of the model. The second is called the *development set* and is used to test the model as we try to improve it. (It is also referred to as the *held-out set* or the *validation set*.) The third is the *test set*. Once the model is fixed and (if we are lucky) producing good results, we then evaluate on the test-set examples. This prevents us from accidentally developing a program that works on the development set but not on yet unseen problems. These sets are sometimes called *corpora*, as in "test corpus." The Mnist data we use is available on the web. The training data consists of 60,000 images and their correct labels, and the development/test set has 10,000 images and labels.

The great property of the perceptron algorithm is that, if there is a set of parameter values that enables the perceptron to classify all the training set correctly, the algorithm is guaranteed to find it. Unfortunately, for most real-world examples there is no such set. On the other hand, even then perceptrons often work remarkably well in the sense that there are parameter settings that label a very high percentage of the examples correctly.

The algorithm works by iterating over the training set several times, adjusting the parameters to increase the number of correctly identified examples. If we get though the training set without any parameters needing to change, we know we have a correct set and we can stop. However, if there is no such set then they continue to change forever. To prevent this we cut off training after N iterations, where N is a system parameter set by the programmer. Typically N grows with the total number of parameters to be learned. Henceforth we will be careful to distinguish between the system parameters Φ and other numbers associated with our program that we might otherwise call "parameters" but are not part of Φ, such as N, the number of iterations though the training set. We call the latter *hyperparameters*. Figure 1.5 gives pseudocode for this algorithm. Note the standard use of Δx as "change in x."

The critical lines here are 2(a)i and 2(a)ii. Here a^k is either 1 or 0, indicating if the image is a member of the class ($a^k = 1$) or not. Thus the first of the two lines says, in effect, if the output of the perceptron is the correct label, do nothing. The second specifies how to change the weight w_i so that, if we were immediately to try this example again, the perceptron would either get it right or at least get it less wrong, namely add

1. set b and all of the $\mathbf{w}$'s to 0.

2. for N iterations, or until the weights do not change

   (a) for each training example $\mathbf{x^k}$ with answer a^k
      i. if $a^k - f(\mathbf{x}^k) = 0$ continue
      ii. else for all weights w_i, $\Delta w_i = (a^k - f(\mathbf{x}^k))x_i$

Figure 1.5: The perceptron algorithm

$(a_k - f(\mathbf{x^k}))x_i^k$ to each parameter w_i.

The best way to see that line 2(a)ii does what we want is to go through the possible things that can happen. Suppose the training example x^k is a member of the class. This means that its label $a^k = 1$. Since we got this wrong, $f(\mathbf{x^k})$ (the output of the perceptron on the kth training example) must have been 0, so $(a^k - f(\mathbf{x^k})) = 1$ and for all i $\Delta w_i = x_i$. Since all pixel values are ≥ 0 the algorithm increases the weights, and next time $f(x^k)$ returns a larger value — it is "less wrong." (We leave it as an exercise for the reader to show that the formula does what we want in the opposite situation — when the example is not in the class but the perceptron says that it is.)

With regard to the bias b, we are treating it as a weight for an imaginary feature x_0 whose value is always 1 and the above discussion goes through without modification.

Let us do a small example. Here we only look at (and adjust) the weights for four pixels, pixels $[7, 7]$ (center of top left corner), $[7, 14]$ (top center), $[14, 7]$, and $[4, 14]$. It is usually convenient to divide the pixel values to make them come out between zero and one. Assume that our image is a zero, so $(a = 1)$, and the pixel values for these four locations are .8, .9, .6, and 0 respectively. Since initially all our parameters are zero, when we evaluate $f(x)$ on the first image $\mathbf{w} \cdot \mathbf{x} + b = 0$, so $f(\mathbf{x}) = 0$, so our image was classified incorrectly and $a(1) - f(\mathbf{x_1}) = 1$. Thus the weight $w_{7,7}$ becomes $(0 + 0.8 * 1) = 0.8$. In the same fashion, the next two w_js become 0.9 and 0.6. The center pixel weight stays zero (because the image value there is zero). The bias becomes 1.0. Note in particular that if we feed this same image into the perceptron a second time, with the new weights it would be correctly classified.

Suppose the next image is not a zero, but rather a one, and the two center pixels have value one and the others zero. First, $b + \mathbf{w} \cdot \mathbf{x} = 1 + .8 *$

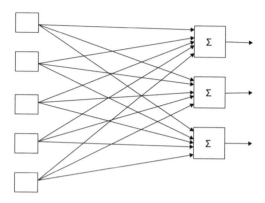

Figure 1.6: Multiple perceptrons for identification of multiple classes

$0 + .9 * 1 + .6 * 0 + 0 * 1 = 1.9$, so $f(x) > 0$ and the perceptron misclassifies the example as a zero. Thus $f(x) - l_x = 0 - 1 = -1$ and we adjust each weight according to line 2(a)ii. $w_{0,0}$ and $w_{14,7}$ are unchanged because the pixel values are zero, while $w_{7,14}$ now becomes $.9 - .9 * 1 = 0$ (the previous value minus the weight times the current pixel value). We leave the new values for b and $w_{14,14}$ to the reader.

We go through the training data multiple times. Each pass through the data is called an *epoch*. Also, note that if the training data is presented to the program in a different order, the weights we learn are different. Good practice is to randomize the order in which the training data is presented each epoch. We come back to this point in Section 1.6. However, for students just coming to this material for the first time, we give ourselves some latitude here and omit this nicety.

We can extend perceptrons to *multiclass decision problems* by creating not just one perceptron, but one for each class we want to recognize. For our original 10-digit problem we would have 10, one for each digit, and then return the class whose perceptron value is the highest. Graphically this is seen in Figure 1.6, where we show three perceptrons for identifying an image as in one of three classes of objects.

While Figure 1.6 looks very interconnected, in actuality it simply shows three separate perceptrons that share the same inputs. Except for the fact

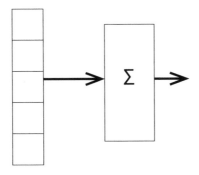

Figure 1.7: NN showing layers

that the answer returned by the multiclass perceptron is the number of the linear unit that returns the highest value, all the perceptrons are trained independently of the others, using exactly the same algorithm shown earlier. So, given an image and label we run the perceptron algorithm step (a) 10 times for the 10 perceptrons. If the label is, say, five but the perceptron with the highest value is six, then the perceptrons for zero to four do not change their parameters (since they correctly said, I am not a zero, or one, etc.). The same is true for six to nine. On the other hand, perceptrons five and six do modify their parameters since they reported incorrect decisions.

1.2   Cross-entropy Loss Functions for Neural Nets

In its infancy, a discussion of neural nets (we henceforth abbreviate as NN) would be accompanied by diagrams much like that in Figure 1.6 with the stress on individual computing elements (the linear units). These days we expect the number of such elements to be large so we talk of the computation in terms of *layers* — a group of storage or computational units that can be thought of as working in parallel and then passing values to another layer. Figure 1.7 is a version of Figure 1.6 that emphasizes this view. It shows an input layer feeding into a computational layer.

Implicit in the "layer" language is the idea that there may be many layers, each feeding into the next. This is so, and this piling of layers is the "deep" in "deep learning."

Multiple layers, however, do not work well with perceptrons, so we need another method of learning how to change weights. In this section we consider how to do this using the next simplest network configuration, *feed-forward neural networks*, and a relatively simple learning technique, *gradient descent*. (Contrariwise, some researchers refer to feed-forward NNs trained with gradient descent as *multilevel perceptrons*.)

Before we can talk about gradient descent, however, we first need to discuss *loss functions*. A loss function is a function from an outcome to how "bad" the outcome is for us. In learning model parameters, our goal is to minimize loss. The loss function for perceptrons has the value zero if we got a training example correct, one if was incorrect. This is known as a *zero-one loss*. Zero-one loss has the advantage of being pretty obvious, so obvious that we never bothered to justify its use. However, it has disadvantages. In particular, it does not work well with gradient descent learning where the basic idea is to modify a parameter according to the rule

$$\Delta\phi_i = -\mathcal{L}\frac{\partial L}{\partial \phi_i} \tag{1.4}$$

Here $\mathcal{L}$ is the *learning rate*, a real number that scales how much we change a parameter at a given time. The important part is the partial derivative of the loss L with respect to the parameter we are adjusting. Or, to put it another way, if we can find how the loss is affected by the parameter in question, we should change the parameter to decrease the loss (hence the minus sign preceding $\mathcal{L}$). In our perceptron, and more generally in NNs, the outcome is determined by Φ, the model parameters, so in such models the loss is a function $L(\Phi)$.

To make this easy to visualize, suppose our perceptron has only two parameters. Then we can think of a Euclidean plane with two axes, ϕ_1 and ϕ_2 and for every point in the plane the value of the loss function hanging over (or under) the point. Say our current values for the parameters are 1.0 and 2.2 respectively. Look at the plane at position $(1, 2.2)$ and observe how L behaves at that point. Figure 1.8, a slice along the plane $\phi_2 = 2.2$, shows how an imaginary loss behaves as a function of ϕ_1. Look at the loss when $\phi_1 = 1$. We see that the tangent line has a slope of about $-\frac{1}{4}$. If the learning rate $\mathcal{L} = .5$, then Equation 1.4 tells us to add $(-.5) * (-\frac{1}{4}) = .125$ — that is, move about .125 units to the right, which indeed decreases the loss.

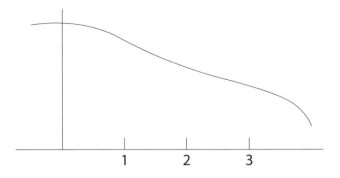

Figure 1.8: Loss as a function of ϕ_1

For Equation 1.4 to work the loss has to be a differentiable function of the parameters, which the zero-one loss is not. To see this, imagine a graph of the number of mistakes we make as a function of some parameter, ϕ. Say we just evaluated our perceptron on an example, and got it wrong. Well, if, say, we keep increasing ϕ (or perhaps decrease it) and we do so enough, eventually $f(x)$ changes its value and we get the example correct. So when we look at the graph we see a step function. But step functions are not differentiable.

There are, however, other loss functions. The most popular, the closest thing to a "standard" loss function, is the *cross-entropy loss* function. In this section we explain what this is and how our network is going to compute it. The subsequent section uses it for parameter learning.

Currently our network of Figure 1.6 outputs a vector of values, one for each linear unit, and we choose the class with the highest output value. We now change our network so that the numbers output are (an estimate of) the probability distribution over classes, in our case the probability that the correct class random variable $C = c$ for $c \in [0, 1, 2, \ldots, 9]$. A *probability distribution* is a set of non-negative numbers that sum to one. Currently our network outputs numbers, but they are generally both positive and negative. Fortunately, there is a convenient function for turning sets of numbers into

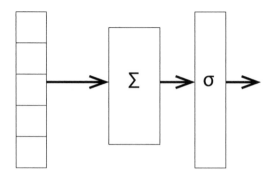

Figure 1.9: A simple network with a softmax layer

probability distributions, *softmax*:

$$\sigma(\mathbf{x})_j = \frac{e^{x_j}}{\sum_i e^{x_i}} \tag{1.5}$$

Softmax is guaranteed to return a probability distribution because even if x is negative e^x is positive, and the values sum to one because the denominator sums over all possible values of the numerator. For example, $\sigma([-1, 0, 1]) \approx [0.09, 0.244, 0.665]$. A special case that we refer to in our further discussion is when all the NN outputs into softmax are zero. $e^0 = 1$, so if there are 10 options all of them receive probability $\frac{1}{10}$, which generalizes naturally to $\frac{1}{n}$ if there are n options.

By the way, "softmax" gets its name from the fact that it is a "soft" version of the "max" function. The output of the max function is completely determined by the maximum input value. Softmax's output is mostly but not completely determined by the maximum. Many machine-learning functions have the name softX for different X but where the outputs are "softened."

Figure 1.9 shows a network with a softmax layer added in. As before, the numbers coming in on the left are the image pixel values; however, now the numbers going out on the right are class probabilities. It is also useful to have a name for the numbers leaving the linear units and going into the softmax function. These are typically called *logits* — a term for un-normalized numbers that we are about to turn into probabilities using softmax. (There seem to be several pronunciations of "logit." The most common seems to be LOW-jit.) We use $\mathbf{l}$ to denote the vector of logits (one for each class). So we have:

$$p(l_i) = \frac{e^{l_i}}{\sum_j e^{l_j}} \tag{1.6}$$

$$\propto e^{l_i} \tag{1.7}$$

Here the second line expresses the fact that, since the denominator of the softmax function is a normalizing constant to make sure the numbers sum to one, the probabilities are proportional to the softmax numerator.

Now we are in a position to define our cross-entropy loss function X:

$$X(\Phi, x) = -\ln p_\Phi(a_x) \tag{1.8}$$

The cross-entropy loss for an example x is the negative log probability assigned to x's label. Or to put it another way, we compute the probabilities of all the alternatives using softmax, then pluck out the one for the correct answer. The loss is the negative log probability of that number.

Let's see why this is reasonable. First, it goes in the right direction. If X is a *loss* function, it should increase as our model gets worse. Well, a model that is improving should assign higher and higher probability to the correct answer. So we put a minus sign in front so that the number gets smaller as the probability gets higher. Next, the log of a number increases/decreases as the number does. So indeed, $X(\Phi, x)$ is larger for bad parameters than for good ones.

But why put in the log? We are used to thinking of logarithms as shrinking distances between numbers. The difference between log(10,000) and log(1000) is 1. One would think that would be a bad property for a loss function: it would make bad situations look less bad. But this characterization of logarithms is misleading. It is true as x gets larger ln x does not increase to the same degree. But consider the graph of –ln(x) in Figure 1.10. As x goes to zero, changes in the logarithm are much larger than the changes to x. And since we are dealing with probabilities, this is the region we care about.

As for why this function is called *cross-entropy loss*, in information theory when a probability distribution is intended to approximate some true distribution, the *cross entropy* of the two distributions is a measure of how

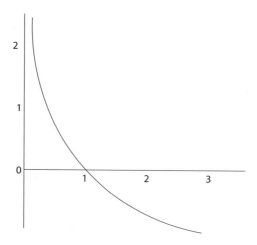

Figure 1.10: Graph of $-\ln x$

different they are. The cross-entropy loss is an approximation of the negative of the cross entropy. As we needn't go any deeper than this into information theory in this book, we leave it with this shallow explanation.

1.3   Derivatives and Stochastic Gradient Descent

We now have our loss function and we can compute it using the following equations:

$$X(\Phi, x) = -\ln p(a) \qquad (1.9)$$

$$p(a) = \sigma_a(\mathbf{l}) = \frac{e^{l_a}}{\sum_i e^{l_i}} \qquad (1.10)$$

$$l_j = b_j + \mathbf{x} \cdot \mathbf{w_j} \qquad (1.11)$$

We first compute the logits $\mathbf{l}$ from Equation 1.11. These are then used by the softmax layer to compute the probabilities (Equation 1.10) and then we compute the loss, the negative natural logarithm of the probability of the correct answer (Equation 1.9). Note that previously the weights for a linear unit were denoted as $\mathbf{w}$. Now we have many such units, so $\mathbf{w_j}$ are the weights for the jth unit and b_j is its bias.

This process, going from input to the loss, is called the *forward pass* of the learning algorithm, and it computes the values that are going to be used in the *backward pass* — the weight adjustment pass. Several methods are used for this. Here we use *stochastic gradient descent*. There term *gradient descent* gets its name from looking at the slope of the loss function (its *gradient*), and then having the system lower its loss (descend) by following the gradient. The learning method as a whole is commonly known as *back propagation*.

We start by looking at the simplest case of gradient estimation, that for one of the biases, b_j. We can see from Equations 1.9–1.11 that b_j changes loss by first changing the value of the logit l_j, which then changes the probability and hence the loss. Let's take this in steps. (In this we are considering only the error induced by a single training example, so we write $X(\Phi, x)$ as $X(\Phi)$.) First:

$$\frac{\partial X(\Phi)}{\partial b_j} = \frac{\partial l_j}{\partial b_j} \frac{\partial X(\Phi)}{\partial l_j} \tag{1.12}$$

This uses the chain rule to say what we said earlier in words — changes in b_j cause changes in X by virtue of the changes they induce in the logit l_j.

Look now at the first partial derivative on the right in Equation 1.12. Its value is, in fact, just 1:

$$\frac{\partial l_j}{\partial b_j} = \frac{\partial}{\partial b_j}(b_j + \sum_i x_i w_{i,j}) = 1 \tag{1.13}$$

where $w_{i,j}$ is the ith weight of the jth linear unit. Since the only thing in $b_j + \sum_i x_i w_{i,j}$ that changes as a function of b_j is b_j itself, the derivative is 1.

We next consider how X changes as a function of l_j:

$$\frac{\partial X(\Phi)}{\partial l_j} = \frac{\partial p_a}{\partial l_j} \frac{\partial X(\phi)}{\partial p_a} \tag{1.14}$$

where p_i is the probability assigned to class i by the network. So this says that since X is dependent only on the probability of the correct answer, l_j affects X only by changing this probability. In turn,

$$\frac{\partial X(\phi)}{\partial p_a} = \frac{\partial}{\partial p_a}(-\ln p_a) = -\frac{1}{p_a} \tag{1.15}$$

(from basic calculus).

This leaves one term yet to evaluate:

$$\frac{\partial p_a}{\partial l_j} = \frac{\partial \sigma_a(\mathbf{l})}{\partial l_j} = \begin{cases} (1 - p_j)p_a & a = j \\ -p_j p_a & a \neq j \end{cases} \tag{1.16}$$

The first equality of Equation 1.16 comes from the fact that we get our probabilities by computing softmax on the logits. The second equality comes from Wikipedia. The derivation requires careful manipulation of terms and we do not carry it out. However, we can make it seem reasonable. We are asking how changes in the logit l_j are going to affect the probability that comes out of softmax. By reminding ourselves that

$$\sigma_a(\mathbf{l}) = \frac{e^{l_a}}{\sum_i e^{l_i}}$$

it makes sense that there are two cases. Suppose the logit we are varying (j) is not equal to a. That is, suppose this is a picture of a 6, but we are asking about the bias that determines logit 8. In this case l_j appears only in the denominator, and the derivative should be negative (or zero) since the larger l_j, the smaller p_a. This is the second case in Equation 1.16, and sure enough, this case produces a number less than or equal to zero since the two probabilities we multiply cannot be negative.

On the other hand, if $j = a$, then l_j appears in both the numerator and denominator. Its appearance in the denominator tends to decrease the output, but in this case it is more than offset by the increase in the numerator. Thus for this case we expect a positive (or zero) derivative, and this is what the first case of Equation 1.16 delivers.

With this result in hand we can now derive the equation for modifying the bias parameters b_j. Substituting Equations 1.15 and 1.16 into Equation 1.14 gives us:

$$\frac{\partial X(\Phi)}{\partial l_j} = -\frac{1}{p_a} \begin{cases} (1 - p_j)p_a & a = j \\ -p_j p_a & a \neq j \end{cases} \tag{1.17}$$

$$= \begin{cases} -(1 - p_j) & a = j \\ p_j & a \neq j \end{cases} \tag{1.18}$$

The rest is pretty simple. We noted in Equation 1.12 that

$$\frac{\partial X(\Phi)}{\partial b_j} = \frac{\partial l_j}{\partial b_j} \frac{\partial X(\Phi)}{\partial l_j}$$

and then that the first of the derivatives on the right has value 1. So the derivative of the loss with respect to b_j is given by Equation 1.14. Last, using the rule for changing weights (Equation 1.12), we get the rule for updating the NN bias parameters:

$$\Delta b_j = \mathcal{L} \begin{cases} (1 - p_j) & a = j \\ -p_j & a \neq j \end{cases} \tag{1.19}$$

The equation for changing weight parameters (as opposed to bias) is a minor variation of Equation 1.19. The equation corresponding to Equation 1.12 for weights is:

$$\frac{\partial X(\Phi)}{\partial w_{i,j}} = \frac{\partial l_j}{\partial w_{i,j}} \frac{\partial X(\Phi)}{\partial l_j} \tag{1.20}$$

First, note that the rightmost derivative is the same as in Equation 1.12. This means that during the weight adjustment phase we should save this result when we are doing the bias changes to reuse here. The first of the two derivatives on the right evaluates to

$$\frac{\partial X(\Phi)}{\partial w_{i,j}} = \frac{\partial}{\partial w_{i,j}}(b_j + (w_{1,j}x_1 + \ldots + w_{i,j}x_i + \ldots)) = x_i \tag{1.21}$$

(Had we taken to heart the idea that a bias is simply a weight whose corresponding feature value is always 1, we could have just derived this equation, and then Equation 1.13 would have followed immediately from 1.21 when applied to this new pseudoweight.)

Using this result yields our equation for weight updates:

$$\Delta w_{i,j} = -\mathcal{L}x_i \frac{\partial X(\Phi)}{\partial l_j} \tag{1.22}$$

We have now derived how the parameters of our model should be adjusted in light of a single training example. The *gradient descent* algorithm would then have us go though all the training examples recording how each would recommend moving the parameter values, but not actually changing them until we have made a complete pass through all of them. At this point we modify each parameter by the sum of the changes from the individual examples.

The problem here is that this algorithm can be very slow, particularly if training set is large. We typically need to adjust the parameters often since they are going to interact in different ways as each increases and decreases as the result of particular test examples. Thus in practice we almost never use gradient descent but rather *stochastic gradient descent*, which updates the parameters every m examples, for m much less that the size of the training set. A typical m might be twenty. This is called the *batch size*.

In general, the smaller the batch size, the smaller the learning rate $\mathcal{L}$ should be set. The idea is that any one example is going to push the weights toward classifying that example correctly at the expense of the others. If the learning rate is low, this does not matter that much, since the changes made to the parameters are correspondingly small. Conversely, with larger batch

1. for j from 0 to 9 set b_j randomly (but close to zero)

2. for j from 0 to 9 and for i from 0 to 783 set $w_{i,j}$ similarly

3. until development accuracy stops increasing

    (a) for each training example k in batches of m examples
        i. do the forward pass using Equations 1.9, 1.10, and 1.11
        ii. do the backward pass using Equations 1.22, 1.19, and 1.14
        iii. every m examples, modify all Φs with the summed updates

    (b) compute the accuracy of the model by running the forward pass on all examples in the development corpus

4. output the Φ from the iteration *before* the decrease in development accuracy.

Figure 1.11: Pseudocode for simple feed-forward digit recognition

size we are implicitly averaging over m different examples, so the dangers of tilting parameters to the idiosyncrasies of one example are lessened and changes made to the parameters can be larger.

1.4   Writing Our Program

We now have the broad sweep of our first NN program. The pseudocode is in Figure 1.11. Starting from the top, the first thing we do is initialize the model parameters. Sometimes it is fine to initialize all to zero, as we did in the perceptron algorithm. While this is so in our current problem as well, it is not always the case. Thus general good practice is to set weights randomly but close to zero. You might also want to give the Python random-number generator a seed so when you are debugging you always set the parameters to the same initial values and thus should get exactly the same output. (If you do not, Python uses a numbers from the environment, like the last few digits from the clock, as the seed.)

Note that at every iteration of the training we first modify the parameters, and then use the model on the development set to see how well it performs with its current set of parameters. When we run development examples we do *not* run the backward training pass. If we were actually going to be using our program for some real purpose (e.g., reading zip codes on mail), the examples we see are not ones on which we have been able to train, and thus we want to know how well our program works "in the wild." Our development data are an approximation to this situation.

A few pieces of empirical knowledge come in handy here. First, it is common practice to have pixel values not stray too far from -1 to 1. In our case, since the original pixel values were 0 to 255, we simply divided them by 255 before using them in our network. This is an instance of a process called *data normalization*. There are no hard and fast rules, but often keeping inputs from -1 to 1 or 0 to 1 makes sense. One place we can see why this is true here is in Equation 1.22 above, where we saw that the difference between the equation for adjusting the bias term and that for a weight coming from one of the NN inputs was that the latter had multiplicative term x_i, the value of the input term. At the time we said that if we had taken to heart our comment that the bias term was simply a weight term whose input value was always 1, the equation for updating bias parameters would have fallen out of Equation 1.22. Thus, if we leave the input values unmodified and one of the pixels has the value 255, we modified its weight value 255 times more than we modify a bias. Given we have no a priori reason to think one needs more correction than the other, this seems strange.

Next there is the question of setting $\mathcal{L}$, the learning rate. This can be tricky. In our implementation we used 0.0001. The first thing to note is that setting it too large is much worse than too small. If you do this you get a math overflow error from softmax. Looking again to Equation 1.5, one of the first things that should strike you are the exponentials in both the numerator and denominator. Raising e (≈ 2.7) to a large value is a foolproof way to get an overflow, which is what we will be doing if any of the logits get large, which in turn can happen if we have a learning rate that is too big. Even if an error message does not give you the striking warning that something is amiss, a too high learning rate can cause your program to wander around in an unprofitable area of the learning curve.

For this reason it is standard practice to observe what happens to the loss on individual examples as the computation proceeds. Let us start with what to expect on the very first training image. The numbers go through the NN and get fed out to the logits layer. All our weights and biases are zero plus or minus a small bit (say .1). This means all the logit values are very close to zero, so all the probabilities are very close to $\frac{1}{10}$. (See the discussion on page 12.) The loss is minus the natural log of the probability assigned to the correct answer, $-\ln(\frac{1}{10}) \approx 2.3$. As a general trend we expect individual losses to decline as we train on more examples. But naturally, some images are further from the norm than others, and thus are classified by the NN with less certainty. Thus we see individual losses that go higher or lower, and the trend may be difficult to discern. Thus, rather than print out one loss at a time, we sum all of them as we go along and print the average every, say, 100 batches. This average should decrease in an easily observable fashion, though even here you may see jitter.

Returning to our discussion of learning rate and the perils of setting it too high, a learning rate that is too low can really slow down the rate at which your program converges to a good set of parameters. So staring small and experimenting with larger values is usually the best course of action.

Because so many parameters are all changing at the same time, NN algorithms can be hard to debug. As with all debugging, the trick is to change as few things as possible before the bug manifests itself. First, remember the point that when we modify weights, if you immediately run the same training example a second time, the loss is less. If this is not true then either there is a bug, or you set the learning rate too high. Second, remember that it is not necessary to change all the weights to see the loss decrease. You can change just one of them, or one group of them. For example, when you first run the algorithm only change the biases. (However, if you think about it, a bias in a one-layer network is mostly going to capture the fact that different classes occur with different frequencies. This does not happen much in the Mnist data, so we do not get much improvement by just learning biases in this case.)

If your program is working correctly you should get an accuracy on the development data of about 91% or 92%. This is not very good for this task. In later chapters we see how to achieve about 99%. But it is a start.

One nice thing about really simple NNs that that sometimes we can directly interpret the values of individual parameters and decide if they are reasonable or not. You may remember that in our discussion of Figure 1.1, we noted that the pixel (8,8) was dark — it had a pixel value of 254. We remarked that this was somewhat diagnostic of images of the digit 7, as opposed to, for example, the digit 1, which would not normally have markings in the upper left-hand corner. We can turn this observation into a prediction about values in our weight matrix $w_{i,j}$, where i is the pixel number and j is the answer value. If the pixel values go from 0 to 784, then the position (8,8) would be pixel $8 \cdot 28 + 8 = 232$, and the weight connecting it to the answer 7 (the correct answer) would be $w_{232,7}$, while that connecting it to 1 would be $w_{232,1}$. You should make sure you see that this now suggests that $w_{232,7}$ should be larger than $w_{232,1}$. We ran our program several times with low-variance random initialization of our weights. In each case the former number was positive (e.g., .25) while the second was negative (e.g., −.17).

1.5 Matrix Representation of Neural Nets

Linear algebra gives us another way to represent what is going on in a NN: using matrices. A *matrix* is a two-dimensional array of elements. In our case these elements are real numbers. The dimensions of a matrix are the number of rows and columns, respectively. So a l by m matrix looks like this:

$$\mathbf{X} = \begin{pmatrix} x_{1,1} & x_{1,2} & \cdots & x_{1,m} \\ x_{2,1} & x_{2,2} & \cdots & x_{2,m} \\ & & \cdots & \\ x_{l,1} & x_{l,2} & \cdots & x_{l,m} \end{pmatrix} \tag{1.23}$$

The primary operations on matrices are addition and multiplication. Addition of two matrices (which must be of the same dimensions) is element-wise. That is, if we add two matrices $\mathbf{X} = \mathbf{Y} + \mathbf{Z}$, then $x_{i,j} = y_{i,j} + z_{i,j}$.

Multiplication of two matrices $\mathbf{X} = \mathbf{YZ}$ is defined when $\mathbf{Y}$ has dimensions l and m and those of $\mathbf{Z}$ are m and n. The result is a matrix of size l by n, where:

$$x_{i,j} = \sum_{k=1}^{k=m} y_{i,k} z_{k,j} \tag{1.24}$$

As a quick example,

$$\begin{pmatrix} 1 & 2 \end{pmatrix} \begin{pmatrix} 1 & 2 & 3 \\ 4 & 5 & 6 \end{pmatrix} + \begin{pmatrix} 7 & 8 & 9 \end{pmatrix} = \begin{pmatrix} 9 & 12 & 15 \end{pmatrix} + \begin{pmatrix} 7 & 8 & 9 \end{pmatrix}$$
$$= \begin{pmatrix} 16 & 20 & 24 \end{pmatrix}$$

We can use this combination of matrix multiplication and addition to define the operation of our linear units. In particular, the input features are a $1 * l$ matrix $\mathbf{X}$. In the digit problem $l = 784$. The weights on the units are $\mathbf{W}$ where $w_{i,j}$ is the ith weight for unit j. So the dimensions of $\mathbf{W}$ are the number of pixels by the number of digits, $784 * 10$. $\mathbf{B}$ is a vector of biases with length 10, and

$$\mathbf{L} = \mathbf{XW} + \mathbf{B} \tag{1.25}$$

where $\mathbf{L}$ is a length 10 vector of logits. It is a good habit when first seeing an equation like this to make sure the dimensions work.

We can now express the loss (L) for our feed-forward Mnist model as follows:

$$\Pr(A(x)) = \sigma(\mathbf{x}\mathbf{W} + \mathbf{b}) \tag{1.26}$$

$$L(x) = -\log(\Pr(A(x) = a)) \tag{1.27}$$

where the first equation gives the probability distribution over the possible classes ($A(x)$), and the second specifies the cross-entropy loss.

We can also express the backward pass more compactly. First, we introduce the *gradient operator*

$$\nabla_{\mathbf{l}} X(\Phi) = \left(\frac{\partial X(\Phi)}{\partial l_1} \cdots \frac{\partial X(\Phi)}{\partial l_m} \right) \tag{1.28}$$

The inverted triangle, $\nabla_{\mathbf{x}} f(\mathbf{x})$, denotes a vector created by taking the partial derivative of f with respect to all the values in $\mathbf{x}$. Previously we just talked about the partial derivative with respect to individual l_j. Here we define the derivative with respect to all of $\mathbf{l}$ as the vector of individual derivatives. We also remind the reader of the transpose of a matrix — making the rows of the matrix into columns, and vice versa:

$$\begin{pmatrix} x_{1,1} & x_{1,2} & \cdots & x_{1,m} \\ x_{2,1} & x_{2,2} & \cdots & x_{2,m} \\ & & \cdots & \\ x_{l,1} & x_{l,2} & \cdots & x_{l,m} \end{pmatrix}^T = \begin{pmatrix} x_{1,1} & x_{2,1} & \cdots & x_{l,1} \\ x_{1,2} & x_{2,2} & \cdots & x_{l,2} \\ & & \cdots & \\ x_{1,m} & x_{2,m} & \cdots & x_{l,m} \end{pmatrix} \tag{1.29}$$

With these we can rewrite Equation 1.22 as

$$\mathbf{\Delta W} = -\mathcal{L}\mathbf{X}^T \nabla_{\mathbf{l}} X(\Phi) \tag{1.30}$$

On the right we are multiplying a $784 * 1$ times a $1 * 10$ matrix to get a $784 * 10$ matrix of changes to the $784 * 10$ matrix of weights $\mathbf{W}$.

This is an elegant summary of what is going on when the input layer feeds into the layer of linear units to produce the logits, which is followed by the loss derivatives propagating back to the changes in the parameters. But there is also a practical reason for preferring this new notation. When run with a large number of linear units, linear algebra in general and deep-learning training in particular can be very time consuming. However, a great many problems can be expressed in matrix notation, and many programming languages have special packages that let you program using linear algebra constructs. Furthermore, these packages are optimized to make them more efficient than if you had coded them by hand. In particular, if you program in

Python it is well worth using the *Numpy* package and its matrix operations. Typically you get an order-of-magnitude speedup.

Furthermore, one particular application of linear algebra is computer graphics and its use in game-playing programs. This has resulted in specialized hardware called *graphics processing units* or *GPUs*. GPUs have slow processors compared to CPUs, but they have a lot of them, along with the software to use them efficiently in parallel for linear algebraic computations. Some specialized languages for NNs (e.g., *Tensorflow*) have built-in software that senses the availability of GPUs and uses them without any change in code. This typically gives another order-of-magnitude increase in speed.

There is yet a third reason for adopting matrix notation in this case. Both the special-purpose software packages (e.g., Numpy) and hardware (GPUs) are more efficient if we process several training examples in parallel. Furthermore, this fits with the idea that we want to process some number m of training examples (the batch size) before we update the model parameters. To this end, it is common practice to input all m of them to our matrix processing to run together. In Equation 1.25 we envisioned the image $\mathbf{x}$ as a matrix of size 1*784. This was one training example, with 784 pixels. We now change this so the matrix has dimensions m by 784. Interestingly, this almost works without any changes to our processing (and the necessary changes are already built into, e.g., Numpy and Tensorflow). Let's see why.

First, consider the matrix multiplication XW where now X has m rows rather than 1. Of course, with one row we get an output of size $1 * 784$. With m rows the output is $m * 784$. Furthermore, as you might remember from linear algebra but can in any case confirm by consulting the definition of matrix multiplication, the output rows are as if in each case we did multiplication of a single row and then stacked them together to get the $m * 784$ matrix.

Adding on the bias term in the equation does not work out so well. We said that matrix addition requires both matrices to have the same dimensions. This is no longer true for Equation 1.25, as $\mathbf{XW}$ now has size m by 10 whereas $\mathbf{B}$, the bias terms, has size 1 by 10. This is where the modest changes come in.

Numpy and Tensorflow have *broadcasting*. When some arithmetic operation requires arrays to have sizes different from the ones they have, arrays dimensions can sometimes be adjusted. In particular, when one of the arrays has dimension $1 * n$ and we require $m * n$, the first gets $m - 1$ (virtual) copies made of its one row or column so that it is the correct size. This is exactly what we want here. This makes $\mathbf{B}$ effectively $m * 10$. So we add the bias to all the terms in the $m * 10$ output from the multiplication. Remember what we did when this was 1 by 10. Each of the 10 was one possible decision for what the correct answer might be, and we added the bias to the number for that decision. Now we are doing the same, but for each possible decision and for all the m examples we are running in parallel.

1.6 Data Independence

All the theorems to the effect that if the following assumptions hold, then our NN models, in fact, converge to the correct solution depend on the *iid assumption* — that our data are independent and identically distributed. A canonical example is cosmic ray measurements — the rays stream in and the processes involved are random and unchanging.

Our data seldom (almost never) look like this — imagine the National Institute of Standards providing a constant stream of new examples. For the data in the first epoch the iid assumption looks pretty good, but as soon as we start on the second, our data are identical to the first time. In some cases our data can fail to be iid starting with training example 2. This is often the case in deep reinforcement learning (deep RL, Chapter 6), and for this reason networks in that branch of deep RL often suffer from *instability* — failure of the net to converge on the correct solution, or sometimes *any* solution. Here we consider a relatively small example where just entering the data in a non-random order can have disastrous results.

Suppose for each Mnist image we added a second that is identical but with black and white reversed — i.e., if the original has a pixel value v, the reversed image has $-v$. We now train our Mnist perceptron on this new corpus, but using different training example orders. (And we assume the batch size is some even integer.) In the first ordering each original Mnist digit image is immediately followed by its reversed version. The claim is (and we verified this empirically) that our simple Mnist NN fails to perform better than chance. A few moments' thought should make this seem reasonable. We see image one, and the backward pass modifies the weights. We now process the second, reversed image. Because the input is minus the previous input and everything else is the same, the changes to all of the weights exactly cancel out the previous ones, and at the end of the training set there are no changes to any of the weights. So no learning, and the same random choices we started with.

On the other hand, there really should not be anything too difficult about learning to handle each data set, regular and reversed, separately and it should be only modestly more difficult for a single set of weights to

handle both. Indeed, simply randomizing the order of input is sufficient
to get performance back to nearly the level of the original problem. If we
see the reverse image, say, 10,000 samples later, the weights have changed
sufficiently so the reverse image does not exactly cancel out the original
learning. If we had an unending source of images and flipped a coin to decide
to feed the NN the original or reversed, then even this small cancelation
would go away.

1.7   References and Further Readings

In this and subsequent "References and Further Readings" sections I try to
do several things more or less simultaneously: (a) point the student to follow-
on material for the chapter topic, (b) identify some important contributions
to the field, and (c) cite references that I myself used to learn this material.
In all cases, particularly (b), I make no claims to completeness or objectivity.
I realized this when in preparation for writing this section I started to read
up on the history of neural nets. In particular I read a blog post by Andrey
Kurenkov [Kur15] to check my memories (and perhaps add to them).

One of the key early papers in NNs was that by McCulloch and Pitts
[MP43], who proposed what we call here a linear unit as a formal model
of a neuron. This is back in 1943. They did not, however, have a learning
algorithm that could train one or more of them to do a task. That was
Rosenblatt's big contribution in his 1958 perceptrons paper [Ros58]. However, as we noted in the text, his algorithm only worked for a single-layer
NN.

The next big step was the invention of back propagation, which *does*
work for multiple-layered NNs. This was one of those situations where many
researchers all came to an idea independently over a period of several years.
(This happens, of course, only when the initial papers do not attract enough
attention that everyone else finds out that the problem had been solved.)
The paper that brought this period to an end was by Rumelhart, Hinton,
and Williams, and it explicitly notes that theirs is a rediscovery [RHW86].
This paper was one of many from a group at University of San Diego that
was responsible for the second flowering of neural networks under the rubric
of *parallel distributed processing (PDP)*. A two-volume collection of these
papers was quite influential [RMG+87].

As for how I learned whatever I know about NNs, I give more specifics in
later chapters. For this chapter I remember very early on reading a blog by
Steven Miller [Mil15] that goes through the forward and backward passes

of back propagation very slowly and with a great numerical example. More generally, let me note two general NN textbooks I have consulted. One is *Deep Learning* by Ian Goodfellow, Yoshua Bengio, and Aaron Courville [GBC16]; the second is *Hands-On Machine Learning with Scikit-Learn and Tensorflow* by Aurélien Géron [Gér17].

1.8 Written Exercises

Exercise 1.1: Consider our feed-forward Mnist program with a batch size of one. Suppose we look at the bias variables before and after training on the first example. If they are being set correctly (i.e., if there are no bugs in our program), describe the changes you should see in their values.

Exercise 1.2: We simplify our Mnist computation by assuming our "image" has two binary-valued pixels, 0 and 1, there are no bias parameters, and we are performing a binary classification problem. (a) Compute the forward-pass logits and probabilities when the pixel values are [0,1], and the weights are:

$$\begin{matrix} .2 & -.3 \\ -.1 & .4 \end{matrix}$$

Here $w[i, j]$ is the weight on the connection between the ith pixel and the jth unit. E.g., $w[0, 1]$ here is $-.3$. (b) Assume the correct answer is 1 (not 0) and use a learning rate of 0.1. What is the loss? Also, compute $\Delta w_{0,0}$ on the backward pass.

Exercise 1.3: Same questions as in Exercise 1.2 except the image is [0,0].

Exercise 1.4: A fellow student asks you, "In elementary calculus we found minima of a function by differentiating it, setting the resulting expression to zero, and then solving the equation. Since our loss function is differentiable, why don't we do that rather than bothering with gradient descent?" Explain why this is not, in fact, possible.

Exercise 1.5: Compute the following:

$$\begin{pmatrix} 1 & 2 \\ 3 & 4 \end{pmatrix} \begin{pmatrix} 0 & 1 \\ 2 & 3 \end{pmatrix} + \begin{pmatrix} 4 & 5 \end{pmatrix} \tag{1.31}$$

You should assume broadcasting so the computation is well defined.

Exercise 1.6: In this chapter we limited ourselves to classification problems, for which cross entropy is typically the loss function of choice. There are also problems where we want our NN to predict particular values. For example, undoubtedly many folks would like a program that, given the price of a particular stock today plus all sorts of other facts about the world, outputs the price of the stock tomorrow. If we were training a single-layer NN to do this we we would typically use the *squared-error loss*:

$$L(\mathbf{X}, \Phi) = (t - l(\mathbf{X}, \Phi))^2 \tag{1.32}$$

where t is the actual price that was achieved on that day and $l(\mathbf{X}, \Phi)$ is the output of the one layer NN with $\Phi = \{\mathbf{b}, \mathbf{W}\}$. (This is also known as *quadratic loss*.) Derive the equation for the derivative of the loss with respect to b_i.

Chapter 2

Tensorflow

2.1 Tensorflow Preliminaries

Tensorflow is an open-source programming language developed by Google that is specifically designed to make programming deep-learning programs easy, or at least easier. We start with the traditional first program:

```
import tensorflow as tf
x = tf.constant("Hello World")
sess = tf.Session()
print(sess.run(x)) #will print out "Hello World"
```

If this looks like Python code, that is because it is. In fact, Tensorflow (henceforth *TF*) is a collection of functions that can be called from inside different programming languages. The most complete interface is from inside Python, and that is what we use here.

The next thing to note is that TF functions do not so much execute a program as define a computation that is executed only when we call the **run** command, as in the last line of the above program. More precisely, the TF function **Session** in the third line creates a session, and associated with this session is a graph defining a computation. Commands like **constant** add elements to this computation. In this case the element is just a constant data item whose value is the Python string "Hello World". The third line tells TF to evaluate the TF variable pointed to by x inside the graph associated with the session **sess**. As you might expect, this results in the printout "Hello World".

It is instructive to contrast this behavior with what happens if we replace the last line with **print(x)**. This prints out:

```
x = tf.constant(2.0)
z = tf.placeholder(tf.float32)
sess= tf.Session()
comp=tf.add(x,z)
print(sess.run(comp,feed_dict={z:3.0}))  # Prints out 5.0
print(sess.run(comp,feed_dict={z:16.0})) # Prints out 18.0
print(sess.run(x)) # Prints out 2.0
print(sess.run(comp)) # Prints out a very long error message
```

Figure 2.1: Placeholders in TF

```
Tensor("Const:0", shape=(), dtype=string)
```

The point is that the Python variable 'x' is not bound to a string, but rather to a piece of the Tensorflow computation graph. It is only when we evaluate this portion of the graph by executing **sess.run(x)** that we access the value of the TF constant.

So, perhaps to belabor the obvious, in the above code 'x' and '**sess**' are Python variables, and as such could have been named whatever we wanted. **import** and **print** are Python functions, and must be spelled this way for Python to understand which function we want executed. Last, **constant**, **Session** and **run** are TF commands and again the spelling must be exact (including the capital "S" in **Session**). Also, we always need first to **import tensorflow**. Since this is fixed we omit it henceforth.

In the code in Figure 2.1, x is again a Python variable whose value is a TF constant, in this case the floating-point number 2.0. Next, z is a Python variable whose value is a TF *placeholder*. A placeholder in TF is like the formal variable in a programming language function. Suppose we had the following Python code:

```
x = 2.0
def sillyAdd(z):
   return z+x
print(sillyAdd(3))  # Prints out 5.0
print(sillyAdd(16)) # Prints out 18.0
```

Here 'z' is the name of **sillyAdd**'s argument, and when we call the function as in **sillyAdd(3)** it is replaced by its value, 3. The TF version works similarly, except the way to give TF placeholders a value is different, as seen in the fifth line of Figure 2.1:

```
print(sess.run(comp,feed_dict={z:3.0})).
```

Here `feed_dict` is a named argument of `run` (so its name must be spelled correctly). It takes as possible values Python dictionaries. In the dictionary each placeholder required by the computation must be given a value. So the first `sess.run` prints out the sum of 2.0 and 3.0, and the second 18.0. The third is there to note that if the computation does not require the placeholder's value, then there is no need to supply it. On the other hand, as the comment on the fourth print statement indicates, if the computation requires a value and it is not supplied you get an error.

Tensorflow is called **Tensor**flow because its fundamental data structures are *tensors* — typed multidimensional arrays. There are fifteen or so tensor types. When we defined the placeholder `z` above we gave its type as a `float32`. Along with its type, a tensor has a *shape*. So consider a $2 * 3$ matrix. It has shape [2, 3]. A vector of length 4 has shape [4]. This is different from a $1 * 4$ matrix, which has shape [1, 4], or a 4 by 1 matrix whose shape is [4, 1]. A 3 by 17 by 6 array has shape [3, 17, 6]. They are all tensors. Scalars (i.e., numbers) have the null shape, and are tensors as well. Also, be aware that tensors do not make the linear-algebra distinction between row vectors and column vectors. There are tensors whose shape has one component, e.g., [5], and that is it. How we draw them on the page is immaterial to the mathematics. When we illustrate array tensors we always obey the rule that the zeroth dimension is drawn vertically and the first horizontally. But that is the limit of our consistency. (Also, note that tensor components are referred to in zero-based counting.)

Returning to our discussion of placeholders: most placeholders are not the simple scalars of our previous examples, but rather multidimensional tensors. For example, the next section starts with a simple Tensorflow program for Mnist digit recognition. The primary TF code will take an image and run the forward NN pass to get the network's guess as to what digit we are looking at. Also, during the training phase it runs the backward pass and modifies the program's parameters. To hand the program the image we define a placeholder. It will be of type `float32` and shape [28,28], or possibly [784], depending on if we handed it a two- or one-dimensional Python list. E.g.,

```
img=tf.placeholder(tf.float32,shape=[28,28])
```

Note that `shape` is a named argument of the `placeholder` function.

One more TF data structure before we dive into the real program. As noted before, NN models are defined by their parameters and the program's architecture — how the parameters are combined with the input values to produce the answer. The parameters (e.g., the weights **w** that connect the input image to the answer logits) are (typically) initialized randomly, and the NN modifies them to minimize the loss on the training data. There are three stages to creating TF parameters. First, create a tensor with initial values. Then turn the tensor into a `Variable` (which is what TF calls parameters) and then initialize the variables/parameter. For example, let's create the parameters we need for the feed-forward Mnist pseudocode in Figure 1.11. First the bias terms b, then the weights W:

```
bt = tf.random_normal([10], stddev=.1)
b = tf.Variable(bt)
W = tf.Variable(tf.random_normal([784,10],stddev=.1))
sess=tf.Session()
sess.run(tf.global_variables_initializer())
print(sess.run(b))
```

The first line adds an instruction to create a tensor of shape [10] whose ten values are random numbers generated from a *normal distribution* with standard deviation 0.1. (A normal distribution, also called a *Gaussian distribution*, is the familiar bell-shaped curve. Numbers picked from a normal distribution will be centered about the mean (μ), and how far they move away from the mean is governed by the *standard deviation* (σ). More specifically, about 68% of the values picked will be within one standard deviation of the mean, and the probability of going further than that decreases rapidly.)

The second line of the above code takes `bt` and adds a piece of the TF graph that creates a variable with the same shape and values. Because we seldom need the original tensor once we have created the variable, normally we combine the two events without saving a pointer to the tensor, as in the third line which creates the parameters W. Before we can use either b or W we need to initialize them in the session we have created. This is done in the fifth line. The sixth line prints out (when I just ran it; it will be different every time):

```
[-0.05206999   0.08943175 -0.09178174 -0.13757218   0.15039739
   0.05112269  -0.02723283 -0.02022207   0.12535755 -0.12932496]
```

If we had reversed the order of the last two lines we would have received an error message when we attempted to evaluate the variable pointed to by b in the print command.

So in TF programs we create variables in which we store the model parameters. Initially their values are uninformative, typically random with small standard deviation. In line with the previous discussion, the backward pass of gradient descent modifies them. Once modified, the session pointed to by `sess` retains the new values, and uses them the next time we run the session.

2.2 A TF Program

In Figure 2.2 we give an (almost) complete TF program for a feed-forward NN Mnist program. It should work as written. The key element that you do not see here is the code `mnist.train.next_batch`, which handles the details of reading in the Mnist data. Just to orient yourself, note that everything before the dashed line is concerned with setting up the TF computation graph; everything after uses the graph first to train the parameters, and then run the program to see how accurate it is on the test data. We now go through this line by line.

After importing Tensorflow and the code for reading in Mnist data, we define our two sets of parameters in lines 5 and 6. This is a minor variant of what we just saw in our discussion of TF variables. Next, we make placeholders for the data we feed into the NN. First, in line 8 we have the placeholder for the image data. It is a tensor of shape `[batchSz, 784]`. In our discussion of why linear algebra was a good way to represent NN compuations (page 23) we noted that our computation speeded up when we process several examples at the same time, and furthermore, this fits nicely with the notion of a batch size in stochastic gradient descent. Here we see how this plays out in TF. Namely, our placeholder for the image takes not one row of 784 pixels, but 100 of them (since this is the value of `batchSz`). Similarly, in line 9 we see that we give the program 100 of the image answers at a time.

One other point about line 9. We represent an answer by a vector of length 10 with all values zero except the ath, where a is the correct digit for that image. For example, we opened Chapter 1 with an image of a 7 (Figure 1.1). The corresponding representation of the correct answer is $(0,0,0,0,0,0,0,1,0,0)$. Vectors of this form are called *one-hot vectors* because they have the property of selecting only one value as active.

Line 9 finishes with the parameters and inputs of our program and our code moves on to placing the actual computations in the graph. Line 11 in particular begins to show the power of TF for NN computations. It defines most of the forward NN pass of our model. In particular it specifies that we want to feed (a batch size of) images into our linear units (as defined

```
0 import tensorflow as tf
1 from tensorflow.examples.tutorials.mnist import input_data
2 mnist = input_data.read_data_sets("MNIST_data/", one_hot=True)
3
4 batchSz=100
5 W = tf.Variable(tf.random_normal([784, 10],stddev=.1))
6 b = tf.Variable(tf.random_normal([10],stddev=.1))
7
8 img=tf.placeholder(tf.float32, [batchSz,784])
9 ans = tf.placeholder(tf.float32, [batchSz, 10])
10
11 prbs = tf.nn.softmax(tf.matmul(img, W) + b)
12 xEnt = tf.reduce_mean(-tf.reduce_sum(ans * tf.log(prbs),
13                                      reduction_indices=[1]))
14 train = tf.train.GradientDescentOptimizer(0.5).minimize(xEnt)
15 numCorrect= tf.equal(tf.argmax(prbs,1), tf.argmax(ans,1))
16 accuracy = tf.reduce_mean(tf.cast(numCorrect, tf.float32))
17
18 sess = tf.Session()
19 sess.run(tf.global_variables_initializer())
20 #-----------------------------------------------
21 for i in range(1000):
22   imgs, anss = mnist.train.next_batch(batchSz)
23   sess.run(train, feed_dict={img: imgs, ans: anss})

25 sumAcc=0
26 for i in range(1000):
27    imgs, anss= mnist.test.next_batch(batchSz)
28    sumAcc+=sess.run(accuracy, feed_dict={img: imgs, ans: anss})
29 print "Test Accuracy: %r" % (sumAcc/1000)
```

Figure 2.2: Tensorflow code for a feed-forward Mnist NN

0.20	0.10	0.20	0.10	0.40		-1.6	-2.3	-1.6	-2.3	-0.9
0.20	0.10	0.20	0.10	0.40	$\rightarrow$	-1.6	-2.3	-1.6	-2.3	-0.9
0.20	0.10	0.20	0.10	0.40		-1.6	-2.3	-1.6	-2.3	-0.9

Figure 2.3: Operation of `tf.log`

0	0	1	0	0		1.6	2.3	1.6	2.3	0.9		0	0	1.6	0	0
0	0	1	0	0	$*$	1.6	2.3	1.6	2.3	0.9	$=$	0	0	1.6	0	0
0	0	0	0	1		1.6	2.3	1.6	2.3	0.9		0	0	0	0	0.9

Figure 2.4: Computation of answers times negative log probabilities

by `W` and `b`) and then apply softmax on all the results to get a vector of probabilities.

We recommend that when looking at code like this, you first check the shapes of the tensors involved to make sure they are sensible. Here the innermost computation is a matrix multiplication `matmul` of the input images [100, 784] times `W` [784, 10] to give us a matrix of shape [100, 10], to which we add the biases, ending up with a matrix of shape [100, 10]. These are the ten logits for the 100 images in our batch. We then pass this through the softmax function and end up with a [100, 10] matrix of label probability assignments for our images.

Line 12 computes the average cross-entropy loss over the 100 examples we process in parallel. Working our way from the inside out, `tf.log(x)` returns a tensor with every element of `x` replaced by its natural log. In Figure 2.3 we show `tf.log` operating on an batch size of three vectors, each with a five-member probability distribution.

Next the standard multiplication symbol "*" in `ans * tf.log(prbs)` does element-by-element multiplication of two tensors. Figure 2.4 shows how element-by-element multiplication of one-hot vectors for each label in the batch times the negative natural-log matrix creates rows in which everything is zeroed out except for the negative log of the probability of the correct answer.

At this point, to get the per-image cross entropy we simply need to sum all the values in the array. The first operation we apply to do this is

```
tf.reduce_sum( A,reduction_indices = [1]),
```

which sums the rows of `A`, as in Figure 2.5. A critical piece here is

```
reduction_indices = [1].
```

In our earlier introduction of tensors we mentioned in passing that dimensions of tensors use zero-based numbering. Now `reduce_sum` can sum over

0	0	1.6	0	0		1.6
0	0	1.6	0	0	$\rightarrow$	1.6
0	0	0	0	0.9		0.9

Figure 2.5: The computation of `tf.reduce_sum` with a reduction index of [1]

columns, the default, with `reduction_index=[0]` or, as in this case, sum over rows, `reduction_index=[1]`. This results in a [100,1] array with the log of the correct probability as the only entry in each row. (Figure 2.5 only uses a batch size of three, and assumes five alternative choices, not 10.) As the last bit of cross-entropy computation, `reduce_mean` in line 13 of Figure 2.2 sums all the columns (again the default) and returns the average (1.1 or thereabouts).

Finally we can move on to line 14 of Figure 2.2, and it is there that TF really shows its merits: this one line is all we need to enable the entire backward pass:

```
tf.train.GradientDescentOptimizer(0.5).minimize(xEnt)
```

This says to compute the weight changes using gradient descent and to minimize the cross-entropy loss function defined in lines 12, and 13. It also specifies a learning rate of .5. We do not have to worry about computing derivatives or anything. If you express the forward computation in TF and the loss in TF, then the TF compiler knows how to compute the necessary derivatives and string them together in the right order to make the changes. We can modify this function call by choosing a different learning rate, or, if we had a different loss function, replace `xEnt` with something that pointed to a different TF computation.

Naturally there are limits to TF's ability to derive the backward pass on the basis of the forward pass. To repeat, it is able to do this only if all the forward-pass computations are done with TF functions. For beginners like us, this is not too great a limitation as TF has a wide variety of built-in operations that it knows how to differentiate and connect.

Lines 15 and 16 compute the **accuracy** of the model. That is, they count the number of correct answers and divide by the number of images processed. First, focus on the standard mathematical function *argmax*, as in $\arg\max_x f(x)$, which returns the value of x that maximizes $f(x)$. In our use here `tf.argmax(prbs,1)` takes two arguments. The first is the tensor over which we are taking the argmax. The second is the *axis* of the tensor to use in the argmax. This works like the named argument we used for `reduce_sum`

— it lets us sum over different axes of the tensor. For example, if the tensor is $((0,2,4),(4,0,3))$ and we use axis 0 (the default) we get back $(1,0,0)$. We first compared 0 to 4 and returned 1 since 4 was larger. We then compared 2 to 0 and returned 0 since 2 was larger. If we had used axis 1 we would have returned $(2,0)$. In line 15 we have a batch-size array of logits. The argmax function returns a batch-size array of maximum logit positions. We next apply `tf.equal` to compare the max logits to the correct answer. It returns a batch-size vector of boolean values (True if they are equal), which `tf.cast(tensor, tf.float32)` turns into floating-point numbers so that `tf.reduce_mean` can add them up and get the percentage correct. Do not cast the boolean values into integers, since when you take the mean it will return an integer as well, which in this case will always be zero.

Next, once we have defined our session (line 18) and initialized the parameter values (line 19), we can train the model (lines 21 to 23). There we use the code we got from the TF Mnist library to extract 100 images and their answers at one time and then run them by calling `sess.run` on the piece of the computation graph pointed to by `train`. When this loop is finished we have trained on 1000 iterations with 100 images per iteration, or 100,000 test images all together. On my four-processor Mac Pro this takes about 5 seconds (more the first time to get the right things into the cache). I mention "four processor" because TF looks at the available computational power and generally does a good job of using it without being told what to do.

Note one slightly odd thing about lines 21 to 23 — we never explicitly mention doing the forward pass! TF figures this out as well, based on the computation graph. From the `GradientDescentOptimizer` it knows that it needs to have performed the computation pointed to by `xEnt` (line 12), which requires the `probs` computation, which in turn specifies the forward-pass computation on line 11.

Last, lines 25 through 29 show how well we do on the test data in terms of percentage correct (91% or 92%). First, just glancing at the organization of the graph, observe that the `accuracy` computation ultimately requires the forward-pass computation `probs` but not the backward pass `train`. Thus, as we should expect, the weights are not modified to perform better on the testing data.

As mentioned in Chapter 1, printing out the error rate as we train the model is good debugging practice. As a general rule it decreases. To do this we change line 23 to

```
acc,ignore= sess.run([accuracy,train],
```

```
feed_dict={img: imgs, ans: anss})
```

The syntax here is normal Python for combining computations. The value of the first computation (that for `accuracy`) is assigned to the variable `acc`, the second to `ignore`. (A common Python idiom would be to replace `ignore` with the underscore symbol (_), the universal Python symbol used when the syntax requires a variable to accept a value but we have no need to remember it.) Naturally we would also need to add a command to print out the value of `acc`.

We have mentioned this to encourage the reader to avoid a common mistake (at least your author and some of his beginning students have made it). The mistake is to leave line 23 alone and add a new line 23.5:

```
acc= sess.run(accuracy, feed_dict={img: imgs, ans: anss}).
```

This, however, is less efficient as TF now does the forward pass twice, once when we tell it to train and once when we ask for the accuracy. And there is a more important reason to avoid this situation. Note that the first call modifies the weights and thus makes the correct label for this image more likely. By placing the request for the accuracy after that the programmer gets an exaggerated idea of how well the program is performing. When we have one call to `sess.run` but ask for both values, this does not happen.

2.3   Multilayered NNs

The program we have designed, in pseudocode in Chapter 1 and just now in TF, is single layered. There is one layer of linear units. The natural question is, can we do better with multiple layers of such units? Early on NN researchers realized that the answer is "No." This follows almost immediately after we see that linear units can be recast as linear algebra matrices — that is, once we see that a one-layer feed-forward NN is simply computing $\mathbf{y} = \mathbf{XW}$. In our Mnist model $\mathbf{W}$ has shape [784, 10] in order to transform the 784 pixel values into 10 logit values and add an extra weight to replace the bias term. Suppose we add an extra layer of linear units $\mathbf{U}$ with shape [784, 784], which in turn feeds into a layer $\mathbf{V}$ with the same shape as $\mathbf{W}$, [784, 10]:

$$\mathbf{y} = (\mathbf{xU})\mathbf{V} \tag{2.1}$$

$$= \mathbf{x}(\mathbf{UV}) \tag{2.2}$$

The second line follows from the associative property of matrix multiplication. The point here is that whatever capabilities are captured in the

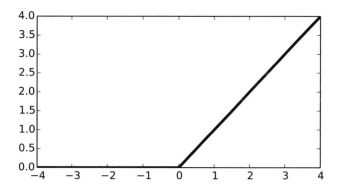

Figure 2.6: Behavior of `tf.nn.relu`

two-layer situation by the combination of **U** followed by the multiplication with **V** could be captured by a one-layer NN with **W** = **UV**.

It turns out there is a simple solution — add some nonlinear computation between the layers. One of the most commonly used is `tf.nn.relu` (or ρ), which stands for *rectified linear unit* and is defined as

$$\rho(x) = \max(x, 0), \tag{2.3}$$

and is shown in Figure 2.6.

Nonlinear functions put between layers in deep learning are called *activation functions*. While relu is currently quite popular, others are in use as well — e.g., the *sigmoid* function, defined as

$$S(x) = \frac{e^{-x}}{1 + e^{-x}} \tag{2.4}$$

and shown in Figure 2.7. In all cases activations are applied piecewise to the individual real numbers in the tensor argument. For example, $\rho([1, 17, -3]) = [1, 17, 0]$.

Before it was discovered that a nonlinearity as simple as relu would work, sigmoid was very popular. But the range of values that sigmoid can output is quite limited, zero to one, whereas relu goes from zero to infinity. This is critical when we do the backward pass to find the gradient of how parameters affect the loss. Back propagation through functions with a limited range of values can make the gradient effectively zero — a process known as the *vanishing gradient* problem. The simpler activation functions have been a great help here. For this reason `tf.nn.lrelu`, *leaky relu*, is also very much

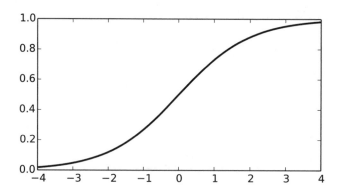

Figure 2.7: The sigmoid function

used because it has a still wider range of values than `relu`, as seen in Figure 2.8.

Putting the pieces of our multilayer NN together, our new model is:

$$\Pr(A(x)) = \sigma(\rho(\mathbf{x}\mathbf{U} + \mathbf{b}_u)\mathbf{V} + \mathbf{b}_v) \tag{2.5}$$

where σ is the softmax function, $\mathbf{U}$ and $\mathbf{V}$ are the weights of the first and second layer of linear units, and $\mathbf{b}_u$ and $\mathbf{b}_v$ are their biases.

Let's now do this in TF. In Figure 2.9 we replace the definitions of $\mathbf{W}$ and $\mathbf{b}$ in lines 5 and 6 from Figure 2.2 with the two layers $\mathbf{U}$ and $\mathbf{V}$, lines 1 through 4 in Figure 2.9. We also replace the computation of `prbs` in line 11 of Figure 2.2 with lines 5 though 7 in Figure 2.9. This turns our code into a multilayered NN. (Also, to reflect the larger number of parameters, we need to lower the learning rate by a factor of 10.) While the old program plateaued at about 92% accuracy after training on 100,000 images, the new one achieves about 94% accuracy on 100,000 images. Furthermore, if we increase the number of training images, performance on the test set keeps increasing to about 97%. Note that the only difference between this code and that without the nonlinear function is line 6. If we delete it, performance indeed goes back down to about 92%. It is enough to make you believe in mathematics!

One other point. In a single-layer network with array parameters $\mathbf{W}$, the shape of $\mathbf{W}$ is fixed by number of inputs on the one hand (784) and the number of possible outputs on the other (10). With two layers there is one more choice we are free to make, the *hidden size*. So $\mathbf{U}$ is input-size by hidden-size and $\mathbf{V}$ is hidden-size by output-size. In Figiure 2.9 we just

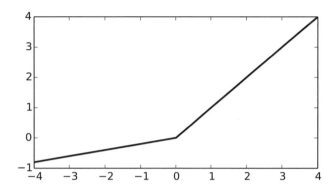

Figure 2.8: The function `lrelu`

```
1 U = tf.Variable(tf.random_normal([784,784], stddev=.1))
2 bU = tf.Variable(tf.random_normal([784], stddev=.1))
3 V = tf.Variable(tf.random_normal([784,10], stddev=.1))
4 bV = tf.Variable(tf.random_normal([10], stddev=.1))
5 L1Output = tf.matmul(img,U)+bU
6 L1Output=tf.nn.relu(L1Output)
7 prbs=tf.nn.softmax(tf.matmul(L1Output,V)+bV)
```

Figure 2.9: TF graph construction code for multilevel digit recognition

set hidden-size to 784, the same as the input size, but nothing required this choice. Typically, making it larger improves performance, but it plateaus.

2.4   Other Pieces

In this section we cover aspects of TF that are very useful when doing the programming assignments suggested in the rest of the book (e.g., checkpointing) or that we use otherwise in the upcoming chapters.

2.4.1   Checkpointing

It is often useful to checkpoint a TF computation — save the tensors in a computation so the computation can be resumed at another time, or for reuse in a different program. In TF we do so by creating and using *saver objects*:

```
saveOb= tf.train.Saver()
```

As before, `saveOb` is Python variable and the choice of name is yours. The object can be created at at any time prior to its use, but for reasons explained below, doing this just before initializing variables (calling `global_variable_initialize`) is a logical place. Then after every n epochs of training, save the current values of all your variables:

```
saveOb.save(sess, "mylatest.ckpt")
```

The `save` method takes two arguments: the session to be saved, and the file name and location. In the above case the information goes in the same directory as the Python program. If the argument had been `tmp/model.checkpt` it would have gone in the `tmp` subdirectory.

The call to `save` creates four files. The smallest, named `checkpoint`, is an Ascii file specifying a few high-level details of the checkpointing that has been done to that directory. The name `checkpoint` is fixed. If you name one of your files "checkpoint" it will be overwritten. The other three file names use the string you gave to `save`. In this case they are named:

```
mylatest.ckpt.data-00000-of-00001
mylatest.ckpt.index
mylatest.chpt.meta
```

The first of these has the parameter values you saved. The other two contain metainformation that TF uses when you want to import these values (as described shortly). If your program calls **save** repeatedly, these files are overwritten each time.

Next we want to, say, do further training epochs on the same NN model we have already started training. The simplest thing to do is to modify the original training program. You retain the creation of the saver object, but now we want to initialize all TF variables with the saved values. Thus, one typically removes **global_variable_initialize** and replaces it with a call to the **restore** method of our saver object:

```
saveOb.restore(sess, "mylatest.ckpt")
```

The next time you call the training program it resumes training with the TF variables set to the values they had when you last saved them in your previous training. Nothing else changes, however. So, if your training code printed out, say, epoch number following by the loss, this time around it will print out epoch numbers starting with one unless you rewrite your code to do otherwise. (Naturally if you want to fix this, or generally make things more elegant, you can, but writing better Python code is not our main concern here.)

2.4.2   tensordot

tensordot is a generalization of matrix multiplication to tensors. We are familiar with standard matrix multiplication, **matmul** from the previous chapter. We can call **tf.matmul(A, B)** when **A** and **B** have the same number of dimensions, say n, the last dimension of **A** has the same size as the second to last dimension of **B**, and the first $n - 2$ dimensions are identical. So if the dimensions of **A** are [2, 3, 4] and those of **B** are [2, 4, 6], then the dimensions of the product are [2, 3, 6]. Matrix multiplication can be thought of as taking repeated dot products. For example, the matrix multiplication

$$\begin{pmatrix} 1 & 2 & 3 \\ 4 & 5 & 6 \end{pmatrix} \begin{pmatrix} -1 & -2 \\ -3 & -4 \\ -5 & -6 \end{pmatrix} \tag{2.6}$$

can be accomplished by taking the dot product of the vectors $< 1, 2, 3 >$ and $< -1, -3, -5 >$ and putting the answer in the top left position in the result matrix. Continuing in this fashion, we take the dot product of the ith row with the jth column, and that is the i, jth value in the answer. So if **A** is the first of the above matrices and **B** is the second, this computation can also be expressed as:

```
tf.tensordot(A, B, [[ 1 ], [ 0 ]])
```

The first two arguments are, of course, the tensors upon which we are operating. The third argument is a two-element list: the first element is a list of dimensions from the first argument, the second element is a corresponding list of dimensions from the second argument. This instructs `tensordot` to take the dot products of these two dimensions. Naturally, the specified dimensions must have equal size if we are to take their dot product. Since the 0th dimension is what we are drawing as rows and the 1st is columns, this says to take the dot products of each of the rows of A with each of the columns of B. `tensordot` places the output dimensions in left-to-right ordering, starting with those of A and then going to those of B. That is, in this case we have the input dimensions [2, 3] followed by [3, 2]. The two dimensions involved in the dot product "disappear" (dimensions 1 and 0) to give an answer with dimensions [2, 2].

Figure 2.10 gives a more complicated example that `matmul` could not handle in one instruction. We have borrowed it from Chapter 5 where the variable names will make sense. Here we look at it just to see what `tensordot` is doing. Without looking at the numbers, just look at the third argument in the `tensordot` function call, `[[ 1 ] [ 0 ]]`. This means we are taking the dot product of the 1 dimension of `encOut` and the 0 dimension of `AT`. This is legal since they both have size 4. That is, we are taking dot product of two tensors with dimensions [2, *4*, 4] and [*4*, 3] respectively. (The numbers in italics are the dimensions which undergo dot product.) Since these dimensions go away after the dot product, the resulting tensor has dimensions [2, 4, 3], which, when we print it out at the bottom of the example, is correct. Briefly descending to the actual arithmetic, we are taking the dot product of the columns in the display of the two tensors. That is, the first dot product is between `[1, 1, 1,-1]` and `[.6, .2, .1, .1]`. The result, .8, appears as the first numeric value in the resulting tensor.

Lastly, `tensordot` is not limited to taking the dot product of a single dimension from each tensor. If the dimensions of A are [2, 4, 4] and those of B are [4, 4] then the operation `tensordot(A, B, [[1,2],[0,1]])` results in a tensor of dimension [2].

2.4.3   Initialization of TF Variables

In Section 1.4 we said that it is generally good practice to initialize NN parameters (i.e., TF variables) randomly but close to zero. In our first TF program (Figure 2.9) we cashed out this injunction with a command like:

```
eo=  ( ((  1, 2, 3, 4),
        (  1, 1, 1, 1),
        (  1, 1, 1, 1),
        ( -1, 0,-1, 0)),
       ((  1, 2, 3, 4),
        (  1, 1, 1, 1),
        (  1, 1, 1, 1),
        ( -1, 0,-1, 0)) )
encOut=tf.constant(eo, tf.float32)

AT = (  ( .6, .25, .25 ),
        ( .2, .25, .25 ),
        ( .1, .25, .25 ),
        ( .1, .25, .25 ) )
wAT = tf.constant(AT, tf.float32)

encAT = tf.tensordot(encOut,wAT,[[1],[0]])
sess= tf.Session()

print sess.run(encAT)
[[[ 0.80000001  0.5         0.5        ]
  [ 1.50000012  1.          1.         ]
  [ 2.          1.          1.         ]
  [ 2.70000005  1.5         1.5        ]]
    ...]
```

Figure 2.10: Example of `tensordot`

```
b = tf.Variable(tf.random_normal([10], stddev=.1))
```

where we assumed that a standard deviation of 0.1 was sufficiently "close to zero."

There is, however, a body of theory and practice on the choice of standard deviations in these case. Here we give a rule called *Xavier initialization*. It is routinely used to set the standard deviation when randomly initializing variables. Let n_i be the number of connections coming into the layer and n_o be the number going out. For the variable W in Figure 2.9 $n_i = 784$, the number of pixels, and $n_o = 10$, the number of alternative classifications. For Xavier initialization we set σ, the standard deviation, as follows:

$$\sigma = \sqrt{\frac{2}{n_i + n_o}} \qquad (2.7)$$

E.g., for W, since the values in question are 784 and 10 we get $\sigma \approx 0.0502$, which we rounded to 0.1. In general the standard deviations recommended might vary between 0.3 for a $10 * 10$ layer and 0.03 for one of $1000 * 1000$. The more input and output values, the lower the standard deviation.

Xavier initialization was originally created be used with the sigmoid activation function (see Figure 2.7). As noted before, $\sigma(x)$ becomes relatively unresponsive to x when x is much below –2 or above +2. That is, if the values fed into a sigmoid are too high or too low, a change in them may have little to no effect on values of the loss. Going in the opposite direction, on the backward pass changes in the loss will have no effect on the parameters that feed into the sigmoid if change in the loss is wiped out by the sigmoid. Instead, we want the *variance* of the ratio between a level's input and output to be about one. Here we are using *variance* in its technical sense: the expected value of the squared difference between the value of a numerically valued random variable and its mean. Also, the *expected value* of a random variable X (denoted $E[X]$) is the probabilistic average of its possible values:

$$E[X] = \sum_x p(X = x) * x. \qquad (2.8)$$

A standard example is the expected value of a roll of a fair six-sided die:

$$E[R] = \frac{1}{6} * 1 + \frac{1}{6} * 2 + \frac{1}{6} * 3 + \frac{1}{6} * 4 + \frac{1}{6} * 5 + \frac{1}{6} * 6 = 3.5 \qquad (2.9)$$

So we want to keep the ratio of the input variance to the output variance to about 1 so the level does not contribute to undue attenuation of the signal by the sigmoid function. This places constraints on how we initialize. We give as a brute fact (you can look up the derivation) that for a linear unit with weight matrix W the variance in the forward pass (V_f) and backward pass (V_b) are respectively:

$$V_f(W) = \sigma^2 \cdot n_i \qquad (2.10)$$
$$V_b(W) = \sigma^2 \cdot n_o \qquad (2.11)$$

where σ is the standard deviation of **W**'s weights. (This makes sense given that the variance of a single Gaussian is (σ^2).) If we set both V_f and V_b to zero and solve for σ we get:

$$\sigma = \sqrt{\frac{1}{n_i}} \qquad (2.12)$$

$$\sigma = \sqrt{\frac{1}{n_o}}. \qquad (2.13)$$

Naturally this has no solution unless the cardinality of the inputs is the same as the outputs. Since more often than not this is *not* the case, we take an "average" between the two values, giving us the Xavier rule

$$\sigma = \sqrt{\frac{2}{n_i + n_o}} \qquad (2.14)$$

There are equivalent equations for other activation functions. With the advent of `relu` and other activation functions that do not saturate as easily as sigmoid, the issue is not as important as it once was. Nevertheless the Xavier rule does give us a good handle on what the standard deviation should be, and the TF versions of it and its relatives are frequently used.

2.4.4   Simplifying TF Graph Creation

Looking back at Figure 2.9, we see that we needed seven lines of code to spell out our two-layer feed-forward network. In the grand scheme of things that is not much — consider what would be required were we programing in Python without TF. However, if we were creating, say, an eight-layer network — and by the end of this book you will be doing just that — that would require twenty-four lines of code or thereabouts.

TF has a handy group of functions, the `layers` module, for more compactly coding very common layered situations. Here we introduce:

```
tf.contrib.layers.fully_connected.
```

A layer is said to be *fully connected* if all its units are connected to all the units in the subsequent layer. All of the layers we use in the first two chapters are fully connected, so it has not been necessary to distinguish between them and networks that lack this property. To define such a layer we typically do the following: (a) create the weights $\mathbf{W}$, (b) create the biases $\mathbf{b}$, (c) do the matrix multiplication and add in the biases, and finally (d) apply an activation function. Assuming we have imported `tensorflow.contrib.layers` as `layers`, this can all be done with the single line:

```
layerOut=layers.fully_connected(layerIn,outSz,activeFn)
```

The above call creates a matrix initialized with Xavier initialization and a vector of zero-initialized biases. It returns `layerIn` times the matrix, plus the biases, to which the activation function specified by `activeFn` has been applied. If you do not specify an activation function it uses `relu`. If you specify `None` as the activation function then no activation is used.

With `fully_connected` we can write all seven lines of Figure 2.9 as:

```
L1Output=layers.fully_connected(img,756)
prbs=layers.fully_connected(L1Output,10,tf.nn.softmax)
```

Note that we specified the use of `tf.nn.softmax` to apply to the output of the second layer by using it as the activation function for the second layer.

Of course, if we have a one-hundred-layer NN and this happens, even writing out 100 calls to `fully_connected` is tedious. Fortunately, we can use Python, or whatever the TF API happens to be, for the specification of our network. To cite a somewhat fanciful example, suppose we wanted to create 100 hidden layers, each one 1 smaller than the previous, where the size of the first is a system parameter. We could write:

```
outpt = input
for i in range(100):
    outpt = layers.fully_connected(outpt, sysParam - i)}
```

This example is silly but the point is serious: pieces of TF graphs can be passed around and operated on in Python like lists or dictionaries.

2.5   References and Further Readings

Tensorflow was started by *Google Brain*, a project within Google originated by two Google researchers, Jeff Dean and Greg Corrado, and Stanford professor Andrew Ng. At this time it was called "DistBelief." When its use moved beyond that one project, Google proper took over further development and hired Geoffrey Hinton from University of Toronto, whom we mentioned in Chapter 1 for his pioneering deep-learning contributions.

Xavier initialization takes its name from the first name of Xavier Glorot, the first author of [GB10], which introduced the technique.

These days Tensorflow is only one of many programming languages aimed at deep-learning programming (e.g., [Var17]). In terms of number of users, Tensorflow is by far the most popular. After that, Keras, a higher-level language built on top of Tensorflow, is second, followed by Caffe, originally developed at University of California, Berkeley. Facebook is now supporting a open-source version of Caffe, Caffe2. Pytorch is a Python interface for Torch, a language that has gained favor in the deep-learning natural-language-processing community.

2.6 Written Exercises

Exercise 2.1: What would be the result if in Figure 2.5 we had instead computed `tf.reduce_sum(A)`, where `A` is the array on the left of the figure?

Exercise 2.2: What is wrong with taking line 14 from Figure 2.2 and inserting it between lines 22 and 23, so that the loop now looks like:

```
for i in range(1000):
    imgs, anss = mnist.train.next_batch(batchSz)
    train = tf.train.GradientDescentOptimizer(0.5).minimize(xEnt)
    sess.run(train, feed_dict={img: imgs, ans: anss})
```

Exercise 2.3: Here is another variation on the same lines of code. Is this OK? If not, why not?

```
for i in range(1000):
    img, anss= mnist.test.next_batch(batchSz)
    sumAcc+=sess.run(accuracy, feed_dict={img:img, ans:anss})
```

Exercise 2.4: In Figure 2.10, what would be the the shape of the tensor output of the operation

```
tensordot(wAT, encOut, [[0],[1]]) ?
```

Explain.

Exercise 2.5: Show the computation that confirms that the first number in the tensor printed out at the bottom of the example in Figure 2.10 (0.8) is correct (to three places).

Exercise 2.6: Suppose `input` has shape [50,10]. How many TF variables are created by the the following:

```
O1 = layers.fully_connected(input, 20, tf.sigmoid) ?
```

What will the standard deviation be for the variables in the matrix created?

Chapter 3

Convolutional Neural Networks

The NNs considered so far have all been *fully connected*. That is, they have the property that all the linear units in a layer are connected to all the linear units in the next layer. However, there is no requirement that NNs have this particular form. We can certainly imagine doing a forward pass where a linear unit feeds its output to only some of the next layer's units. Slightly harder, but not all that hard, is seeing that, say, Tensorflow, if it knows which units are connected to which, can correctly compute the weight derivatives on the backward pass.

One special case of partially connected NNs is *convolutional neural networks*. Convolutional NNs are particularly useful in computer vision, and so we continue with our discussion of the Mnist data set.

The one-level fully connected Mnist NN learns to associate particular light intensities at certain positions in the image with certain digits — e.g., high values at position (8,14) with the number 1. But this is clearly not how people work. Photographing the digits in a brighter room might add 10 to each pixel value, but would have little if any influence on our categorization — what matters in scene recognition is differences in pixel values, not their absolute values. Furthermore, the differences are only meaningful between nearby values. Suppose you are in a small room lit by a single lightbulb in one corner of the room. What we perceive as a light patch on, say, some wallpaper at the opposite end of the room could, in fact, be reflecting back fewer photons than a "dark" patch near the bulb. What matters in sorting out what is going on in a scene is local light intensity differences, with the emphasis on "local" and "differences." Naturally computer vision

$$
\begin{array}{cccc}
1.0 & 1.0 & 1.0 & 1.0 \\
1.0 & 1.0 & 1.0 & 1.0 \\
-1.0 & -1.0 & -1.0 & -1.0 \\
-1.0 & -1.0 & -1.0 & -1.0
\end{array}
$$

Figure 3.1: A simple filter for horizontal line detection

researchers are quite aware of this and the standard response to these facts has been the near universal adoption of convolutional methods.[1]

3.1   Filters, Strides, and Padding

For our purposes a *convolutional filter* (also called a *convolutional kernel*) is a (typically small) array of numbers. If we are dealing with a black and white image it is a two-dimensional array. Mnist is black and white, so that is all we need here. If we had color we would need a three-dimensional array — or equivalently three two-dimensional arrays — one each for red, blue, and green (RBG) wavelengths of light, from which it is possible to reconstruct all colors. For the moment we ignore the complications of color. We come back to them later.

Consider the convolution filter shown in Figure 3.1. To *convolve* a filter with a patch of an image we take the dot product of the filter and an equal-size piece of the image. You should remember that the dot product of two vectors does pairwise multiplication of the corresponding elements of the vectors and sums the products to get a single number. Here we are generalizing this notion to arrays of two or more dimensions, so we multiply the corresponding elements of the arrays and then sum all the products.

More formally, we consider the convolution kernel to be a function, the *kernel function*. We get the value V of this function at a position x, y on an image I as follows:

$$
V(x, y) = (I \cdot K)(x, y) = \sum_m \sum_n I(x + m, y + n) K(m, n) \tag{3.1}
$$

That is, formally, convolution is an operation (here represented by a center dot) that takes two functions, I and K, and returns a third function that

---

[1]The discussion here uses the term "convolution" as it is used in deep learning. This is close to but not exactly the same as its use in mathematics, where deep-learning convolution would be called *cross-correlation*.

$$
\begin{array}{cccccc}
0.0 & 0.0 & 0.0 & 0.0 & 0.0 & 0.0 \\
0.0 & 2.0 & 2.0 & 2..0 & 0.0 & 0.0 \\
0.0 & 2.0 & 2.0 & 2..0 & 0.0 & 0.0 \\
0.0 & 2.0 & 2.0 & 2..0 & 0.0 & 0.0 \\
0.0 & 0.0 & 0.0 & 0.0 & 0.0 & 0.0 \\
0.0 & 0.0 & 0.0 & 0.0 & 0.0 & 0.0 \\
\end{array}
$$

Figure 3.2: Image of a small square

performs the operation on the right. For our usual purposes we can skip the formal definition and just go to the right-hand-side operations. Also, we normally think of the point x, y as at or near the middle of the patch we are working on, so for the $4 * 4$ kernel shown above both m and n might vary from -2 up to and including $+1$.

Let us convolve the filter in Figure 3.1 with the lower right-hand piece of the simple image of a square shown in Figure 3.2. The bottom two rows of the filter all overlap with zeros in the image. But the filter's top left four elements all overlap with the 2.0s of the square, so the value of the filter on this patch is 8. Naturally, if all the pixel values were zero the filter application value would be zero. But if the entire image patch were all 10s, it would still be zero. In fact, it is not hard to see that this filter has highest values for patches with a horizontal line running through the middle of the patch going from high values on the top and lower values below. The point, of course, is that filters can be made to be sensitive to changes in light intensities rather than their absolute values and, because filters are typically much smaller than complete images they concentrate on local changes. We can, of course, designe a filter kernel that has high values for image patches with straight lines going from upper left to lower right, or whatever.

In the above discussion we have presented the filter as if it were designed by the programmer to pick out a particular kind of feature in the image, and indeed, this is what was done before the advent of deep convolutional filtering. However, what makes deep-learning approaches special is that *the filter's values are NN parameters — they are learned during the backward pass*. In our current discussion of how convolution works it is easier to ignore this and we continue to present our filters "predesigned" until the next section.

Besides convolving a filter with an image *patch*, we also speak of convolving a filter with an *image*. This involves applying the filter to many of

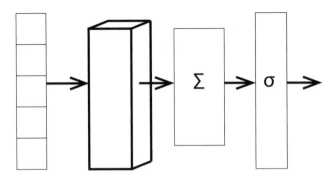

Figure 3.3: An image recognition architecture with convolution filters

the patches in the image. Usually we have a lot of different filters, and the goal of each filter is to pick up a specific feature in the image. Having done this, we can then feed all the feature values to one or more fully connected layers and then into softmax and hence to the loss function. This architecture is shown in Figure 3.3. There we represent the convolution filter layer as a three-dimensional box (because a bank of filters is (at least) a three-dimensional tensor, height by width by number of different filters).

Notice the deliberate vagueness above when we said we convolve a filter with "many" of the patches in an image. To begin to make this more precise, we first define *stride* — the distance between two applications of a filter. A stride of, say, two would mean that we apply a filter at every other pixel. To make this still more specific we talk of both horizontal stride, s_h, and vertical stride, s_v. The idea is that as we go across the image we apply the filter after every s_h pixels. When we reach the end of a line we descend vertically s_v lines and repeat the process. When we apply a filter using a stride of two we still apply the filter to all pixels in the region (not, e.g., only every other one). The only thing affected by the stride is where the filter is next applied.

Next we define what we mean by the "end of a line" in applying a filter. This is done by specifying the *padding* for the convolution. TF allows two possible paddings, *Valid* and *Same* paddings. After convolving the filters

0	1		23	24	25	26	27
.	.	3.2	3.1	2.5	2..0	0	0
.	.	3.2	3.1	2.5	2.0	0	0
.	.	3.2	3.1	2.5	2.0	0	0
.	.	3.2	3.1	2.5	2..0	0	0
.	.	3.2	3.1	2.5	2.0	0	0

Figure 3.4: End of line with Valid and Same padding

with a particular patch of the image we move s_h to the right. There are three possibilities: (a) we are nowhere near the image boundary, so we continue working on this line, (b) the leftmost pixel for the next convolution patch is beyond the image edge, and (c) the leftmost pixel the filters look at is in the image, but the rightmost is beyond the end of the image. Same padding stops in case (b), Valid stops in case (c). For example, Figure 3.4 shows the situation where our image is 28 pixels wide, our filter is 4 pixels wide by 2 pixels high, and our stride is 1. With Valid padding, we stop after pixel 24 with zero-based counting. This is because our stride would take us to pixel 25, and to fit in a filter of width 4 would require a 29th pixel, which does not exist. Same padding would continue to convolve until after pixel 27. Naturally, we make the same choice in the vertical direction when we reach the bottom of the image.

The decision on where to stop is called *padding* because when going horizontally with Same padding, by the time we stop we have to be using "imaginary" pixels. The left-hand side of the filter is within the image boundary, but the right-hand side is not. In TF the imaginary pixels have value zero. So with Same padding we need to pad the boundary of the image with imaginary pixels. With Valid padding almost never do we need actual padding since we stop convolving before any part of the filter moves beyond the image edge. When padding is required (with Same padding), the padding is applied to all edges as equally as possible.

Since we are going to need this later we give the number of patch convolutions we apply horizontally for Same padding:

$$\lceil i_h/s_h \rceil \tag{3.2}$$

where $\lceil x \rceil$ is the *ceiling function*. It returns the smallest integer $\geq x$. To see that we need the ceiling function, consider the case when the image is

an odd number of pixels wide, say five, and the stride is two. First the filter
is applied to the patch 0–2 in the horizontal direction. Then it moves two
positions to the right and is applied to 2–4. When we get to position 4,
it should be applied to 4–6. Since the width is 5, there is no position 6.
However, for Same padding we add a zero to the end of the line to let the
filter work on positions 4–6, and the total number of applications is 4. If
Same padding did not add the extra zeros, the above equation would have
the floor function rather than ceiling. Naturally the same reasoning applies
in the vertical direction, giving us $\lceil i_v/s_v \rceil$.

For Valid padding the number horizontally is

$$\lfloor (i_h - f_h + 1)/s_h \rfloor \tag{3.3}$$

If you don't see this last equation immediately, first make sure you see that
$i_h - f_h$ is how often you can shift (before running out of space) if the stride
is one. But the number of applications is one plus the number of shifts.

Despite its use of imaginary pixels, Same padding is quite popular because when combined with stride of one, it has the property that the size of
the output is the same as that of the original image. Frequently we combine
many layers of convolution, each output becoming the input for the next
layer. No matter what the stride size, valid padding always has an output
smaller than the input. With repeated convolution layers the result gets
eaten away from the outside in.

Before moving on to actual code we need to discuss how convolution
affects how we represent images. The heart of a convolutional NN in TF is
the two-dimensional convolution function

```
tf.nn.conv2d(input, filters, strides, padding)
```

plus optional named arguments that we ignore here. The **2d** in the name
specifies that we are convolving an image. (There are also **1d** and **3d** versions
that convolve one-dimensional objects, such as an audio signal, or for 3d,
perhaps a video clip.) As you might expect, the first argument is a batch
size of individual images. So far we have thought of an individual image
as a 2D array of numbers — each number a light intensity. If you include
the fact that we have batch size of them, the input is a three-dimensional
tensor.

But **tt.nn.conv2d** requires individual images to be three-dimensional
objects where the last dimension is a vector of *channels*. As mentioned
earlier, normal color images have three channels — one each for red, blue,
and green (RBG). From now on when we discuss images, we are still talking

$$(1, -1, -1) \quad (1, -1, -1) \quad (1, -1, -1) \quad (1, -1, -1)$$
$$(-1, 1, 1) \quad (-1, 1, 1) \quad (-1, 1, 1) \quad (-1, 1, 1)$$
$$(-1, 1, 1) \quad (-1, 1, 1) \quad (-1, 1, 1) \quad (-1, 1, 1)$$

Figure 3.5: A simple filter for horizontal ketchup line detection

about a 2D array of pixels, but each pixel is a list of intensities. That list has one value in it for black and white pictures, three values for colored ones.

The same is true for convolution filters. A $m * n$ filter matches up with m by n pixels, but now both the pixels and the filter may have multiple channels. In a somewhat fanciful case, we create a filter to find horizontal edges of ketchup bottles in Figure 3.5. The topmost row of the filter is activated most highly when the input light is intense only for red, and less intense for blue and green. The next two rows want less red (so there is some contrast) and more blue and green.

Figure 3.6 shows a simple TF example of applying a small convolution feature to a small invented image. As noted above, the first input to `conv2D` is a 4D tensor, here the constant `I`. In the comment just before declaring `I` we show what it would look like as a simple 2D array, without the extra dimensions added by batch size (here one) and channel size (again one). The second argument is a 4D tensor of filters, here `W`, again with a comment showing a 2D version, this time without the extra dimensions of number of channels and number of filters (one each). We then show the call to `conv2D` with horizontal and vertical strides both one and Valid padding. Looking at the result, we see that it is 4D [batchSz(1), height(2), width(2), channels(1)]. The height and width are much reduced from the image size, as we should expect when we use Valid padding, and also the filter is quite active (with a value of 6), again as we would expect since it is designed to pick up vertical lines, which are exactly what appear in the image.

3.2 A Simple TF Convolution Example

We now go through the exercise of turning the feed-forward TF Mnist program of Chapter 2 into a convolutional NN model. The code we create is given in Figure 3.7.

As already noted, the key TF function call is `tf.nn.conv2d`. In Figure 3.7 we see in line 5

```
ii = [[ [[0],[0],[2],[2]],
        [[0],[0],[2],[2]],
        [[0],[0],[2],[2]],
        [[0],[0],[2],[2]] ]]
''' ((0 0 2 2)
     (0 0 2 2)
     (0 0 2 2)
     (0 0 2 2))'''
I = tf.constant(ii, tf.float32)

ww = [ [[[-1]],[[-1]],[[1]]],
       [[[-1]],[[-1]],[[1]]],
       [[[-1]],[[-1]],[[1]]] ]
'''((-1 -1 1)
    (-1 -1 1)
    (-1 -1 1))'''
W = tf.constant(ww, tf.float32)

C =  tf.nn.conv2d( I, W, strides=[1, 1, 1, 1], padding='VALID')
sess = tf.Session()
print sess.run(C)
'''[ [[ 6.]   [ 0.]]
     [[ 6.]   [ 0.]]]]'''
```

Figure 3.6: A simple exercise using conv2D

```
1  image = tf.reshape(img, [100, 28, 28, 1])
2      #Turns img into 4d Tensor
3  flts=tf.Variable(tf.truncated_normal([4,4,1,4],stddev=0.1))
4      #Create parameters for the filters
5  convOut = tf.nn.conv2d(image, flts, [1, 2, 2, 1], "SAME")
6      #Create graph to do convolution
7  convOut= tf.nn.relu(convOut)
8      #Don't forget to add nonlinearity
9  convOut=tf.reshape(convOut,[100, 784])
10     #Back to  100 1d image vectors
11 prbs = tf.nn.softmax(tf.matmul(convOut, W) + b)
```

Figure 3.7: Primary code needed to turn Figure 2.2 into a convolutional NN

```
convOut = tf.nn.conv2d(image, flts, [1, 2, 2, 1], "SAME")
```

We look at each argument in turn. As just discussed, image is a four-dimensional tensor — in this case a vector of three-dimensional images. We choose batch size to be 100, so tf.nn.conv2d wants 100 3D images. The functions that read the data in Chapter 2 read in vectors of one-dimensional images (of length 784), so line 1 of Figure 3.7

```
image = tf.reshape(img,[100, 28, 28, 1])
```

converts the input to shape [100, 28, 28, 1], where the final "1" indicates we have only one input channel. tf.reshape works pretty much like Numpy reshape.

The next argument to tf.nn.conv2d in line 5 is a pointer to the filters to be used. This too is a 4D tensor, this time of shape

[height, width, channels, number]

The filter parameters are created in line 3. We have chosen 4 by 4 filters ([4,4]), each pixel has one channel ([4,4,1]), and we have chosen to make four filters ([4,4,1,4]). Note that the filter height and width, and how many we create, are all hyperparameters. The number of channels (in this case 1) is determined by the number of channels in the image, so is fixed. Very importantly, we have finally done what we promised at the beginning — line 3 creates the filter values as parameters of the NN model (with initial values mean zero and standard deviation 0.1), so they are learned by the model.

The *strides* argument to `tf.nn.conv2d` is a list of four integers indicating the stride size in each of the four dimensions of *input*. In line 5 we see we have chosen strides of 1, 2, 2 and 1. In practice the first and last are almost always 1. At any rate, it is hard to imagine a case where they would not be 1. After all, the first dimension is the separate 3D images in the batch. If the stride along this dimension were two, we would be skipping every other image! Equally odd, if the last stride were greater than one, let's say two, and we had three color channels, then we would look only at the red and blue light, skipping green. So typical values for *stride* would be (1, 1, 1, 1), or if we want to convolve only every other image patch in both the horizontal and vertical directions, (1, 2, 2, 1). This is why you often see in discussions of `tf.nn.conv2d` instructions to the effect that the first and last strides must be one.

The final argument, *padding*, is a string equal to one of the padding types TF recognizes, e.g., `SAME`.

The output of `conv2d` is a lot like the input. It too is a 4D tensor, and like the input the first dimension of the output is the batch size. Or in other words, the output is a vector of convolution outputs, one for each input image. The next two dimensions are the number of filter applications, horizontally followed by vertically; these can be determined as in Equations 3.2 and 3.3. The last dimension of the output tensor is the number of filters being convolved with the image. Above we said we would use four. That is, the output shape is

[*batch-size, horizontal-size, vertical-size, number-filters*]

In our case this is going to be (100, 14, 14, 4). If we think of the output as a sort of "image," then the input is 28 by 28 with one channel, but the output is (14 by 14) and 4 channels. This means that in both cases an input image is represented by 784 numbers. We chose this deliberately to keep things similar to Chapter 2, but we need not have done so. We could have, say, chosen to have 16, rather than four, different filters, in which case we would have an image represented by (14*14*16= 3136) numbers.

In line 11 we feed these 784 values into a fully connected layer that produces logits for each image, which in turn are fed into softmax, and we then compute the cross-entropy loss (not shown in Figure 3.7) and we have a very simple convolutional NN for Mnist. The code has the general shape of that in Figure 2.2. Also, line 7 above puts a nonlinearity between the output of the convolution and the input of the fully connected layer. This is important. As seen before, without nonlinear activation functions between linear units one does not get any improvement.

The performance of this program is significantly better than that of Chapter 2's — 96% or a bit more, depending on the random initialization (compared to 92% for the feed-forward version). The number of model parameters is virtually the same for the two versions. The feed-forward layer in both uses 7840 weights in **W** and 100 biases in **b** (784 + 10 weights in each unit in the fully connected layer, times 10 units). Convolution adds four convolution filters, each with 4*4 weights, or 64 more parameters. This is why we set the convolution output size at 784. To a zeroth approximation the quality of an NN goes up as we give it more parameters to use. Here, however, the number of parameters has essentially remained constant.

3.3   Multilevel Convolution

As stated earlier, we can improve the accuracy still further by going from one layer of convolution to several. In this section we construct a model with two layers.

The key point in multilevel convolution is one we made in passing in discussing the output from `tf.conv2d`: it has the same format as the image input. Both are batch size vectors of 3D images, and the images are 2D plus one extra dimension for the number of channels. Thus the output from one layer of convolution can be the input to a second layer, and that is exactly what one does. When we talk of the place-holder image coming from the data, the last dimension is the number of color channels. When we talk of the `conv2d` output, we say the last dimension is the number of different filters in the convolution layer. The word "filter" here is a good one. After all, to let only blue light through a lens we literally put a colored filter in front. So three filters give us images in the RBG spectra. Now we get "images" in pseudospectra like the "horizontal line-boundary spectra." This would be the imaginary image produced by the filter of, e.g., Figure 3.1. Furthermore, just as filters for images with RBG have weights associated with all three spectra, the second convolution layer has weights for each channel output from the first.

We give the code for turning the feed-forward Minst NN into a two-layer convolution model in Figure 3.8. Lines 1–4 are repeats of the first lines of Figure 3.7 except in line 2 we increase the number of filters in the first convolution layer to 16 (from 4 in the earlier version). Line 2 is responsible for creating the second convolution layer filters `flts2`. Note that we created 32 of them. This is reflected in Line 5, where the values of the 32 filters become the 32 input channel values to the second convolution layer.

```
1 image = tf.reshape(img, [100, 28, 28, 1])
2 flts=tf.Variable(tf.normal([4, 4, 1, 16], stddev=0.1))
3 convOut = tf.nn.conv2d(image, flts, [1, 2, 2, 1], "SAME")
4 convOut= tf.nn.relu(convOut)
5 flts2=tf.Variable(tf.normal([2, 2, 16, 32], stddev=0.1))
6 convOut2 = tf.nn.conv2d(convOut, flts2, [1, 2, 2, 1], "SAME")
7 convOut2 = tf.reshape(convOut2, [100, 1568])
8 W = tf.Variable(tf.normal([1568,10],stddev=0.1))
9 prbs = tf.nn.softmax(tf.matmul(convOut2, W) + b)
```

Figure 3.8: Primary code needed to turn Figure 2.2 into a two-layer convolutional NN

When we linearize these output values in line 7 there are (784*4) of them. Remember we started with 784 pixels, and each convolution layer used stride 2, both horizontally and vertically. So the resulting 3D image dimensions after the first convolution were (14, 14, 16). The second convolution also had stride two on the 14 by 14 image and had 32 channels, so the output is [100, 7, 7, 32] and the linearized version of a single image in line 7 has $7 * 7 * 32 = 1568$ scalar values, which is then also the height of W that turns these image values into 10 logits.

Stepping back from the details, note the overall flow of the model. We start with a $28 * 28$ picture. At the end we have a $7 * 7$ "picture," but we also have 32 different filter values at each point in the 2D array. Or, to put it another way, at the end we have split out image into 49 patches, where each patch was initially $4 * 4$ pixels and is now characterized by 32 filter values. Since this improves performance, we are entitled to assume that these values are saying important things about what is going on in their corresponding $4 * 4$ patch.

Indeed, this seems to be the case. While at first glance the actual values in the filters can be baffling, at least at the beginning levels study can reveal some logic in their "construction." Figure 3.9 shows the $4 * 4$ weights for four of the eight first-level convolution filters in that were learned in one run of the code in Figure 3.7. You might spend a few seconds on them to see if you can make out what they are looking for. For some you might. Others do not make much sense to me. However, cross correlating with Figure 3.10 should help. Figure 3.10 was created by printing out, for our now standard image of a 7, the filter with the highest value for all 14 by 14 points in the image after the first convolution layer. Fairly quickly the impression of a 7 emerges from a fog of zeros, so filter 0 is associated with a region of all

```
-0.152168 -0.366335 -0.464648 -0.531652
 0.0182653 -0.00621072 -0.306908 -0.377731
 0.482902  0.581139  0.284986  0.0330535
 0.193956  0.407183  0.325831  0.284819

 0.0407645  0.279199  0.515349  0.494845
 0.140978  0.65135  0.877393  0.762161
 0.131708  0.638992  0.413673  0.375259
 0.142061  0.293672  0.166572 -0.113099

 0.0243751  0.206352  0.0310258 -0.339092
 0.633558  0.756878  0.681229  0.243193
 0.894955  0.91901  0.745439  0.452919
 0.543136  0.519047  0.203468  0.0879601

 0.334673  0.252503 -0.339239 -0.646544
 0.360862  0.405571 -0.117221 -0.498999
 0.520955  0.532992  0.220457  0.000427301
 0.464468  0.486983  0.233783  0.101901
```

Figure 3.9: Filters 0, 1, 2, and 7 of the eight filters created in one run of the two-layer convolution NN

```
0 0 0 0 0 0 0 0 0 0 0 0 0 0
0 0 0 0 0 0 0 0 0 0 0 0 0 0
0 0 0 0 0 0 0 0 0 0 0 0 0 0
0 0 5 2 2 2 2 2 2 2 2 2 0 0
0 0 1 1 4 4 4 4 2 2 2 0 0
0 0 1 1 1 1 1 1 1 2 7 0 0
0 0 0 0 0 0 5 1 4 2 7 0 0
0 0 0 0 0 0 5 1 2 7 0 0 0
0 0 0 0 0 0 5 1 4 2 7 0 0 0
0 0 0 0 0 5 2 1 2 7 0 0 0 0
0 0 0 0 0 5 1 4 2 0 0 0 0 0
0 0 0 0 5 1 4 2 7 0 0 0 0 0
0 0 0 0 2 1 2 2 0 0 0 0 0 0
0 0 0 0 1 1 1 7 0 0 0 0 0 0
```

Figure 3.10: Most active feature for all 14 by 14 points in layer 1 after processing Figure 1.1

zeros. We can then note that the right-hand edge of the 7's diagonal is pretty much all 7s, whereas the bottom of the horizon pieces in the image corresponds to 1s. Look again at the filter values. To me, the 1s, 2s and 7s seem to fit the results in Figure 3.9. On the other hand, there is nothing in filter 0 to suggest blank. However, this too makes sense. We used Numpy's arg-max function, which returns the position of the largest number in a list of numbers. All the pixel values for the blank regions are zero, so all the filters return 0. If the arg-max function returns the first value in the case when all values are equal, this is what we would expect.

Figure 3.11 is similar to Figure 3.10 except it shows the most active filters in layer 2 of the model. It is less interpretable than layer 1. There are various arguments for why this might be the case. We include it mostly because the first convolutional layer of illustrations is much more interpretable than most, but we should not assume that what we saw for layer 1 is typical.

3.4   Convolution Details

3.4.1   Biases

We can also have biases with our convolution kernels. We have not mentioned this until now because it is only in the last example that multiple

```
 0  0  0  0  0  0  0
17 11 31 17 17 16 16
 6 16 12  6  6  5  5
17 17 17  5 24  5 10
 0  0 11 26  3  5  0
 0 17 11 24  5 10  0
 0  6 24  8  5  0  0
```

Figure 3.11: Most active features for all 7 by 7 points in layer 2 after processing Figure 1.1

filters have been applied to each patch, i.e., we specified 16 different filters in line 2 of Figure 3.8. A bias can cause the program to give more or less weight to one filter channel than another by adding in a different value to the channel's convolution output. Thus the number of bias variables at a particular convolution layer is equal to the number of output channels. For example, in Figure 3.8 we could add biases to the first convolution layer by adding the following between lines 3 and 4:

```
bias = tf.Variable(tf.zeros [16])
convOut += bias
```

Broadcasting is implicit. While `convOut` has shape [100, 14,1 4, 16], `bias` has shape [16], so the addition implicitly creates [100, 14, 14] copies of it.

3.4.2 Layers with Convolution

Section 2.4.4 showed how one standard component of NN architectures, fully connected layers, could be written efficiently using `layers`. There are equivalent functions for convolutional layers:

```
tf.contrib.layers.conv2d(inpt,numFlts, fltDim, strides, pad)
```

plus optional named arguments. For example, lines 2 through 4 in Figure 3.8 can be replaced with

```
convOut = layers.conv2d(image,16, [4,4], 2,"Same") ?
```

The convolution output is pointed to by `convOut`. As before, we create 16 different kernels, each with dimensions 4*4. Strides in both directions are two, and we use Same padding. This is not quite identical to the non-`layers` version since `layers.conv2d` assumes you want biases unless you tell it otherwise. If we insist on no biases we simply give a value to the appropriately named argument use_bias=False.

3.4.3   Pooling

As you might expect for larger pictures (e.g., $1000 * 1000$ pixels), the reduction in image size between the original image and the values fed to a fully connected layer, followed by softmax at the end, is much more extreme. There are TF functions that can help handle this reduction. Note in our program that the reduction was because the strides in convolution only looked at every other patch. We could have done the following instead:

```
convOut = tf.nn.conv2d(image, flts, [1,1,1,1], "SAME")
convOut = tf.nn.max_pool(convOut, [1,2,2,1], [1,2,2,1], "SAME").
```

These two lines are intended to replace line 3 in Figure 3.8. Instead of a convolution with stride two, we first applied convolution with stride one. Thus convOut is of shape [batchSz, 28, 28, 1] — no reduction in image size. The next line gives us a reduction in image size exactly equal to that produced by the stride of two we originally used.

The key function here, max_pool, finds the maximum value for a filter over a region in the image. It takes four arguments, with three of the four the same as conv2d. The first is our standard 4D tensor of images, the third the strides, and the last the padding. In the above case max_pool is looking at convOut, the 4D output of the first convolution. It is doing so with strides [1, 2, 2, 1]. The first element of the list says to look at every image in the batch size, and the last says to look at every channel. The two 2s say move two units over before doing the operation again, and do this both horizontally and vertically. The second argument specifies the size of the region over which it is to find the maximum. As usual, the first and last 1s are pretty much forced, while the middle two 2s specify that we are to take the maximum over a $2 * 2$ patch of convOut.

Figure 3.12 contrasts the two different ways we can achieve a factor of four dimensionality reduction in our Mnist program, though here we do it on a $4 * 4$ image. (The numbers are invented.) In the top row we applied the filter with stride two (Same padding) and immediately got the $2 * 2$ array of filter values. In the second row we applied the filter with stride one that creates a $4 * 4$ array of values. Then for each separate $2 * 2$ patch, we output the highest value that gives us the final array on the lower right of the figure.

Before moving on, we note that there is also avg_pool, which works identically to max_pool, except that the value for a pool is the average of

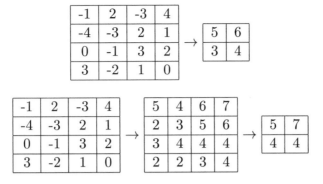

Figure 3.12: Factor of 4 dimensionality reduction, with and without `max_pool`

the individual values, not the maximum.

3.5 References and Further Readings

The paper that introduced the learning of convolutional kernels though NNs and back propagation is by Yann LeCun et al. [LBD+90], although a later, much more complete exploration of the topic, also by LeCun et al. [LBBH98], is the definitive reference. Part of my education in convolutional NNs was provided by Google's tutorial on Mnist digit recogntion [Ten17b].

If you find the idea of getting NNs that can recognize images really neat and want a next project to work on, I would recommend the CFAIR 10 dataset (Canadian Institute for Advanced Research) [KH09]. It too is a ten-way image classification task, but the objects to recognize are more complicated (airplane, cat, frog), the images are in color, the backgrounds can be complicated, and the object to classify is not nicely centered. The image sizes are also larger [32, 32, 3]. The dataset can be downloaded from [Kri09]. The total number of images is about that of Mnist — 60,000, so the total data imprint is manageable. There is also an online Google tutorial on building a NN for this task [Ten17a].

If you are *really* ambitious you could try working on the Imagenet Large Scale Visual Recognition Challenge data set (*ILSVRC*). This is much more difficult. There are 1000 image types, including such classics as french fries or mashed potatoes. This for the last six or seven years has been the dataset used by serious computer vision researchers in an annual competition. For NNs the big year was 2012 when the *Alexnet* deep learning program won the competition — the first time an NN program had won. The program, by Alex Krizhevsky, Ilya Sutskever, and Geoffrey Hinton [KSH12], achieved a *top-5 score* of 15.5% — 15.5% of the time the correct label was not one of the top five answers as scored by the program's assessment of the probability that a particular label is the correct one. The second-place contestant scored 26.2%. Since 2012 all first-place finishers have NNs.

2012	15.5
2013	11.2
2014	6.7
2015	3.6
Human	5–10

Here the "Human" entry indicates that people perform in the 5 to 10% range at this task depending on training.

Tables and charts with the above information are common presentation points when explaining the impact of deep learning on artificial intelligence over the last 10 years or so.

3.6   Written Exercises

Exercise 3.1: (a) Design a $3 * 3$ kernel that detects vertical lines in a black and white image, and returns the value 8 when applied to the upper-left-hand side of the image in Figure 3.2. It should return zero if all the pixels in the patch are of equal intensity. (b) Design another such kernel.

Exercise 3.2: In our discussion of Equation 3.2 we said in an off-hand comment that the size of the convolution filter had no impact on the number of applications when using Same padding. Explain how this can be.

Exercise 3.3: In our discussion of padding we said that Valid padding *always* yields an output image having smaller 2D dimensions than the input. Strictly speaking, this is not the case. Explain the (relatively uninteresting) case when this statement is false.

Exercise 3.4: Suppose the input to a convolution NN is a $32 * 32$ color image. We want to apply eight convolution filters to it, all with shape $5 * 5$. We are using Valid padding and a stride of two both vertically and horizontally. (a) What is the shape of the variable in which we store the filters' values? (b) What is the shape of the output of `tf.nn.conv2d`?

Exercise 3.5: Explain what the following code does differently from the almost identical code at the beginning of Section 3.4.3:

```
convOut = tf.nn.conv2d(image, flts, [1,1,1,1], "SAME")
convOut = tf.nn.maxpool(convOut, [1,2,2,1], [1,1,1,1], "SAME").
```

In particular, for an arbitrary values of `image` and `flts`, does `convOut` have same shape, in both cases? Does it necessarily have the same values? Is one set of values a proper subset of the other? In each case, why or why not?

Exercise 3.6: (a) How many variables are created when we execute the following `layers` command?

```
layers.conv2d(image,10, [2,4], 2, "Same", use_bias=False).
```

Assume `image` has shape [100, 8, 8, 3]. Which of these shape values are irrelevant to the answer? (b) How many are irrelevant if `use_bias` is set to **True** (the default)?

Chapter 4

Word Embeddings and Recurrent NNs

4.1 Word Embeddings for Language Models

A *language model* is a probability distribution over all strings in a language. At first blush this is a hard notion to get your head around. For example, consider the previous sentence "At first blush. . . ." There is a good chance you have never seen this particular sentence, and unless you reread this book you will never see it a second time. Whatever its probability, it must be very small. Yet contrast that sentence with one having the same words but in reverse order. That is still less likely by a huge factor. So strings of words can be more or less reasonable. Furthermore, programs that want to, say, translate Polish into English need to have some ability to distinguish between sentences that sound like English and those that do not. A language model is a formalization of this idea.

We can get some further purchase on the concept by breaking the strings into individual words and then asking, what is the probability of the next word given the previous ones? So let $\mathbf{E_{1,n}} = (E_1 \ldots E_n)$ be a sequence of n random variables denoting a string of n words and $\mathbf{e_{1,n}}$ be one candidate value. E.g., if n were 6 then perhaps $\mathbf{e_{1,6}}$ is (We live in a small world) and we could use the chain rule in probability to give us:

$$P(\text{We live in a small world}) = P(\text{We})P(\text{live}|\text{We})P(\text{in}|\text{We live}) \ldots \quad (4.1)$$

More generally:

$$P(E_{1,n} = e_{1,n}) = \prod_{j=1}^{j=n} P(E_j = e_j | E_{1,j-1} = e_{1,j-1}). \qquad (4.2)$$

Before we go on, we should back up a bit to where we mentioned "break-ing the strings into a sequence of words." This is called *tokenization,* and if this were a book on text understanding we might spend a chapter on this by itself. However, we have different fish to fry, so we simply say that a "word" for our purposes is any sequence of characters between two white spaces (where we consider a line feed as a white space). Note that this means that, e.g., "1066" is a word in the sentence "The Norman invasion happened in 1066." Actually, this is false: according to our definition of "word," the word that appears in the above sentence is "1066."—that is, "1066" with a period after it. So we also assume that punctuation (e.g., periods, commas, colons) is split off from words, so that the final period becomes a word in its own right, separate from the "1066" word that preceded it. (You may now be beginning to see how we might spend an entire chapter on this.)

Also, we are going to cap our English vocabulary at some fixed size, say 10,000 different words. We use V to denote our vocabulary and $|V|$ its size. This is necessary because by the above definition of "word" we should expect to see words in our development and test sets that do not appear in the training set — e.g., "132,423" in the sentence "The population of Providence is 132,423." We do this by replacing all words not in V (so-called *unknown words*) by a special word "*UNK*". So this sentence would now appear in our corpus as "The population of Providence is *UNK* ."

The data we are using in this chapter is known as the *Penn Treebank Corpus,* or the *PTB* for short. The PTB consists of about 1,000,000 words of news articles from the *Wall Street Journal.* It has been tokenized but not "unked," so the vocabulary size is close to 50,000 words. It is called a "treebank" because all the sentences have been turned into trees that show their grammatical structure. Here we ignore the trees as we are only interested in the words. We also replace all words that occur 10 times or less by *UNK*.

With that out of the way, let us return to Equation 4.2. If we had a very large amount of English text we might be able to estimate the first two or three probabilities on its right-hand side simply by counting how often we see, e.g., "We live" and how often "in" appears next, and then dividing the second by the first (i.e., use the maximum likelihood estimate) to give us an estimate of, e.g., $P(\text{in}|\text{We live})$. But as n gets large this is impossible for lack of any examples in the training corpus of a particular, say, fifty-word sequence.

One standard response to this problem is to assume that the probability of the next word depends only on the previous one or two words, so that we can ignore all the words before that when estimating the probability of the next. The version where we assume words depend only on the previous word looks like this:

$$P(E_{1,n} = e_{1,n}) = P(E_1 = e_1) \prod_{j=2}^{j=n} P(E_j = e_j | E_{j-1} = e_{j-1}) \qquad (4.3)$$

This is called a *bigram model*, where "bigram" means "two word." It is called this because each probability depends only on a sequence of two words. We can simplify this equation if we put a imaginary word "STOP" at the beginning of the corpus, and then after every sentence. This is called *sentence padding*. So if the first "STOP" is e_0 Equation 4.3 becomes

$$P(E_{1,n} = e_{1,n}) = \prod_{j=1}^{j=n} P(E_j = e_j | E_{j-1} = e_{j-1}) \qquad (4.4)$$

Henceforth we assume that all our language corpora are sentence padded. Thus, except for the first STOP, our language model predicts all the STOPs as well as all the real words.

With the simplifications we have put it place, it should be clear that creating a bad language model is trivial. If, say, $|V| = 10,000$ we can take the probability of any word coming after any other as $\frac{1}{10000}$. What we want, of course, is a good one — one in which if the last word is "the", the distribution assigns very low probability to "a" and a much higher one to, say, "cat". We do this using deep learning. That is, we give the deep network a word w_i and expect as output a reasonable probability distribution over possible next words.

To start, we need somehow to turn words into the sorts of things that deep networks can manipulate, i.e., floating-point numbers. The now standard solution is to associate each word with a vector of floats. These vectors are called *word embeddings*. For each word we initialize its embedding as a vector of e floats, where e is a system hyperparameter. An e of 20 is small, 100 common, and 1000 not unknown. Actually, we do this in two steps. First, every word in the vocabulary V has a unique index (an integer) from 0 to $|V| - 1$. We then have an array $\mathbf{E}$ of dimensions $|V|$ by e. $\mathbf{E}$ holds all the word embeddings so that if, say, "the" has index 5, the 5th row of $\mathbf{E}$ is the embedding of "the."

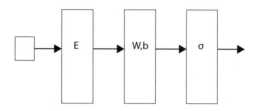

Figure 4.1: A feed-forward net for language modeling

With this in mind, a very simple feed-forward network for estimating the probability of the next word is shown in Figure 4.1. The small square on the left is the input to the network — the integer index of the current word, e_i. On the right are the probabilities assigned to possible next words e_{i+1}, and the cross-entropy loss function is $-\ln P(e_c)$, the negative natural log of the probability assigned to the correct next word. Returning to the left again, the current word is immediately translated into its embedding by the *embedding layer* which looks up the e_ith row in $\mathbf{E}$. From that point on all NN operations are on the word embedding.

A critical point is that $\mathbf{E}$ is a parameter of the model. That is, initially the numbers in $\mathbf{E}$ are random with mean zero and small standard deviation, and their values are modified according to stochastic gradient descent. More generally, in the backward pass Tensorflow starts with the loss function and works backward, looking for all parameters that affect the loss. $\mathbf{E}$ is one such parameter, so TF modifies it. What is amazing about this, aside from the fact that the process converges to a stable solution, is that the solution has the property that words that behave in similar ways end up with embeddings that are "close together." So if e (the size of the embedding vector) is, say, 30, then the prepositions "near" and "about" point in roughly the same direction in 30-dimensional space, and neither is very close to, say, "computer" (which is closer to "machine").

Word Numbers	Word	Largest Cosine Similarity	Most Similar
0	under		
1	above	0.362	0
2	the	−0.160	0
3	a	0.127	2
4	recalls	0.479	1
5	says	0.553	4
6	rules	−0.066	4
7	laws	0.523	6
8	computer	0.249	2
9	machine	0.333	8

Figure 4.2: Ten words, the largest cosine similarity to the previous words, and the index of the word with highest similarity

With a bit more thought, however, perhaps this is not so amazing. Let us think more closely about what happens to embeddings as we try to minimize loss. As already stated, the loss function is the cross-entropy loss. Initially all the logit values are about equal since all the model parameters are about equal (and close to zero).

Now, suppose we had already trained on the pair of words "says that". This would cause the model parameters to move in such a way that the embedding for "says" leads to a higher probability for "that" coming next. Now consider the first time the model sees the word "recalls", and say that furthermore it too is followed by a "that". One way to modify the parameters to make "recalls" predict "that" with higher probability is to have its embedding become more similar to that for "says" since it too wants to predict "that" as the next word. This is indeed what happens. More generally, two words that are followed by similar words get similar embeddings.

Figure 4.2 shows what happens when we run our model on about a million words of text, a vocabulary size of about 7,500 words and an embedding size of 30. The *cosine similarity* of two vectors is a standard measure of how close two vectors are to each another. In the case of two-dimensional vectors it is the standard cosine function and is 1.0 if the vectors point in the same direction, 0 if they are orthogonal and −1.0 if in opposite directions. The computation for arbitrary-dimension cosine similarity is

$$\cos(\mathbf{x}, \mathbf{y}) = \frac{\mathbf{x} \cdot \mathbf{y}}{(\sqrt{(\sum_{i=1}^{i=n} x_i^2)}(\sqrt{(\sum_{i=1}^{i=n} y_i^2)})} \tag{4.5}$$

Figure 4.2 shows five pairs of similar words numbered from zero to nine.

For each word we compute its cosine similarity with all the words that precede it. Thus we would expect all odd-numbered words to be most similar to the word that immediately precedes them, and that is indeed the case. We would also expect even-numbered words (the first of each similar-word pairs) not to be very similar to any of the previous words. For the most part this is true as well.

Because embedding similarity to a great extent mirrors meaning similarity, embeddings have been studied a lot as a way to quantify "meaning" and we now know how to improve this result by quite a bit. The main factor is simply how many words we use for training, though there are other architectures that help as well. However, most methods suffer from similar limitations. For example, they are often blind when trying to distinguish between synonyms and antonyms. (Arguably "under" and "above" are antonyms.) Remember that a language model is trying to guess the next word, so words that have similar next words get similar embeddings, and very often antonyms do exactly that. Also, getting good models for embeddings of phrases is much hard than for single words.

4.2   Building Feed-Forward Language Models

Now let us build a TF program for computing bigram probabilities. It is very similar to the digit recognition model in Figure 2.2 as in both cases we have a single fully connected feed-forward NN ending in a softmax to produce the probabilities needed for a cross-entropy loss. There are only a few differences.

First, rather than an image, the NN takes a word index i where $0 \leq i < |V|$ as input, and the first thing is to replace it by $\mathbf{E}[i]$, the word's embedding:

```
inpt=tf.placeholder(tf.int32, shape=[batchSz])
answr=tf.placeholder(tf.int32, shape=[batchSz])
E = tf.Variable(tf.random_normal([vocabSz, embedSz],
                                    stddev = 0.1))
embed = tf.nn.embedding_lookup(E, inpt)
```

We assume that there is unshown code that reads in the words and replaces the characters by unique word indices. Furthermore this code packages up batchSz of them in a vector. inpt points to this vector. The correct answer for each word (the next word of the text) is a similar vector, answr. Next we created the embedding lookup array E. The function `tf.nn.embedding_lookup` creates the necessary TF code and puts it into the computation graph. Future manipulations (e.g., `tf.matmul`) then operate on `embed`. Naturally, TF can determine how to update `E` to lower the loss, just like the other model parameters.

Turning to the other end of the feed-forward network, we use a built-in TF function to compute the cross-entropy loss:

```
xEnt =  tf.nn.sparse_softmax_cross_entropy_with_logits
                (logits=logits,labels=answr)
loss = tf.reduce_sum(xEnt)
```

The TF function `tf.nn.sparse_softmax_cross_entropy_with_logits` takes two named arguments. Here the `logits` argument (which we conveniently named `logits`) is a `batchSz` of logit values (i.e., a `batchSz` by `vocabSz` array of logits). The `labels` argument is a vector of correct answers. The function feeds the logits into `softmax` to get a column vector of probabilities `batchSz` by `vocabSz`. That is, $s_{i,j}$, the i,jth element of softmax, is the probability of word j in the ith example in that batch. The function then locates the probability of the correct answer (from `answr`) for each line, computes its natural log and outputs a `batchSz` by 1 array (effectively a column vector) of those log probabilities. The second line above takes that column vector and sums it to get the total loss for that batch of examples.

If you are curious, the use of the word "sparse" here is the same as (and presumably taken from) that in, e.g., *sparse matrix*. A sparse matrix is one with very few nonzero values, so it is space efficient to store only the position and values of the nonzero values. Going back to our computation of loss in the first TF Mnist program (page 33), we assumed the correct labels for the digit images were provided in the form of one-hot vectors with only the position of the correct answer nonzero. In `tf.nn.sparse_softmax` we just give the correct answer. The correct answer can be thought of as a sparse version of the one-hot representation.

Returning to the language model with this code in hand, we do a few epochs over our training examples and get embeddings that demonstrate word similarities like those in Figure 4.2. Also, if we want to evaluate the language model we can print out the total loss on the training set after every epoch. It should decrease with increasing epoch number.

In Chapter 1 (page 20) we suggested that within training epochs we print out the average per-example loss, since if our parameters are improving the model, the loss should decrease (the numbers we see should get smaller). Here we suggest a minor tweak on this idea. First, note that in language modeling an "example" is assigning probabilities to possible next words, so the number of training examples is the number of words in our training corpus. So rather than talk about average per-example loss we talk about *average per-word loss*. Next, rather than print out average per-word loss, print out e raised to this power. That is, for a corpus d with $|d|$ words, if the total loss is x_d, then print out:

$$f(d) = e^{\frac{x_d}{|d|}}. \tag{4.6}$$

This is called the *perplexity* of the corpus d. It is a good number to think about because it actually has a somewhat intuitive meaning: on average guessing the next word is equivalent to guessing the outcome of tossing a fair die with that number of outcomes. Note what this means for guessing the second word of our training corpus given the first word. If our corpus has a vocabulary size of 10,000 and we start with all our parameters near zero, then the 10,000 logits on the first example are zero and all the probabilities are 10^{-4}. Readers should confirm that this results in a perplexity that is exactly the vocabulary size. As we train the perplexity decreases, and, for the particular corpus your author used with a vocabulary size of about 7,800 words, after two training epochs with a training set of about 10^6 words the development set had perplexity 180 or so. With a four-CPU laptop the model took about 3 minutes per epoch.

4.3   Improving Feed-Forward Language Models

There are many ways to improve the language model we just developed. For example, in Chapter 2 we saw that adding a hidden layer (with an activation function between the two layers) improved our Mnist performance from 92% correct to 98%. Adding a hidden layer here improves the development set perplexity from 180 to about 177.

But the most straightforward way to get better perplexity is to move from a bigram language model to a *trigram model*. Remember that in going from Equation 4.2 to Equation 4.4 we assumed that the probability of a word depends only on the previous word. Obviously this is false. In general, the choice of the next word can be influenced by words arbitrarily far back, and the influence of the word two back is very large. So a properly trained model that bases its guess on the two previous words (called a *trigram* model because probabilities are based upon sequences of three words) gets much better perplexity than bigram models.

In our bigram model we had one placeholder for the previous word index, `inpt`, and one for the word to predict (assuming a batch size of one) `answr`. We now introduce a third placeholder that has the index of the word two back, `inpt2`. In the TF computation graph we add a node that finds the embedding of `inpt2`,

```
embed2 = tf.nn.embedding_lookup(E, inpt2),
```

and then one for concatenating the two:

```
both= tf.concat([embed,embed2],1)
```

Here the second argument specifies which axis of the tensor has the concatenation done to it. (Remember, in reality we are doing a batch-size of embeddings at the same time, so each of the results of the lookups is a matrix of size batch-size times embedding-size. We want to end up with a matrix of batch-size times (embedding-size *2), so the concatenation happens along axis 1, the rows (remember, the columns are axis 0). Lastly, we need to change the dimensions of **W** from embedding-size * vocabulary-size to (embedding-size * 2) *vocabulary-size.

In other words, we input the embeddings for two previous words, and the NN uses both in estimating the probability of the next word. Furthermore, the backward pass updates the embeddings of both words. This lowers the perplexity from 180 to about 140. Adding yet another word to the input layer lowers things still more, to about 120.

4.4 Overfitting

In Section 1.6 we discussed the iid assumption that lurks behind all the guarantees that the training methods of our NNs do, in fact, lead to good weights. In particular, we noted that as soon as we use our training data for more than one epoch all bets are off.

But aside from a rather contrived example, we offered no empirical evidence on this point. The reason is that the data we used in our Chapter 1 examples, Mnist, is, as data sets go, very well behaved. What we want from training data, after all, is that it covers all the possible things that might occur (and in the correct proportions), so when we look at the testing data there are no surprises. With only ten digits and 60,000 training examples, Mnist meets this criterion quite well.

Unfortunately, most data sets are not that complete, and written-language data sets in general (and the Penn Treebank in particular) are far from ideal.

Epoch	1	2	3	4	5	6	7	10	15	20	30
Train	197	122	100	87	78	72	67	56	45	41	35
Dev	172	152	145	143	143	143	145	149	159	169	182

Figure 4.3: Overfitting in a language model

Epoch	1	2	3	4	5	6	7	10	15	20	30
Dropout	213	182	166	155	150	144	139	131	122	118	114
L2 Reg	180	163	155	148	144	140	137	130	123	118	112

Figure 4.4: Language-model perplexity when using regularization

Even if we restrict vocabulary size to 8,000 words and only look at trigram models, there is a large number of trigrams in the test set that do not appear in the training data. At the same time, repeatedly seeing the same (relatively small) set of examples causes the model to overestimate their probability. Figure 4.3 shows perplexity results for a two-layer trigram language model trained on the Penn Treebank. The rows give the number of epochs we have trained for and the average perplexity for each training example at each epoch, followed by the average over the development corpus.

First, looking at the row of training perplexity, we see that it decreases monotonically with increasing epoch. This is as it should be. The row of development perplexities tells a more complicated story. It too starts out decreasing, from 172 on the first epoch to 143 on the fourth, but then it holds steady for two epochs, and starting on the seventh epoch it increases. By the 20th iteration it is up to 169, and it reaches 182 on the 30th. The difference between the training and development results on the 30th epoch, 35 vs. 182, is classic overfitting of the training data.

Regularization is the general term for modifications to fix overfitting. The simplest regularization technique is *early stopping*: we just stop training at the point where the development perplexity is the lowest. But while simple, early stopping is not the best method for correcting an overfitting problem. Figure 4.4 shows two much better solutions, *dropout* and *L2 regularization*.

In dropout we modify the network to randomly drop pieces of our computation. For example, the dropout data in Figure 4.4 came from randomly dropping the output of 50% of the the first layer of linear units. So the next layer sees zeros in random locations in its input vector. One way to think of this is that the training data no longer is identical at each epoch, since each time different units are dropped. Another way to see why this helps is to note that the classifier cannot depend on the coincidence of a lot of features of the data lining up in a particular way, and thus it should generalize better. As we can see from Figure 4.4, it really does help prevent overfitting. For one thing, the first line of Figure 4.4 shows no reversal in the perplexity of the development corpus. Even at 30 epochs perplexity is decreasing, albeit at a glacier-like rate (about 0.1 units per epoch). Furthermore, the absolute lower value using dropout is much better than we can achieve by early stopping — a perplexity of 114 vs. 145.

The second technique we showcase in Figure 4.4 is L2 regularization. L2 starts from the observation that overfitting in many kinds of machine learning is accompanied by the learning parameters getting quite large (or quite small for weights below zero). We commented earlier that seeing the same data repeated times causes the NN to overestimate the probabilities of what it has seen at the expense of all the examples that could occur, but did not, in the training data. This overestimation is achieved by weights with large absolute values or, almost equivalently, large squared values. In L2 regularization we add to the loss function a quantity proportional to the sum of the squared weights. That is, if before we were using cross-entropy loss, our new loss function would be:

$$\mathcal{L}(\Phi) = -log(\Pr(c)) + \alpha \frac{1}{2} \sum_{\phi \in \Phi} \phi^2 \qquad (4.7)$$

Here α is a real number that controls how we weight the two terms. It is usually small; in the above experiments we set it to .01, a typical value. When we differentiate the loss function with respect to ϕ, the second term adds $\alpha\phi$ to the total of $\frac{\partial \mathcal{L}}{\partial \phi}$. This encourages both positive and negative ϕ to move closer to zero.

Both forms of regularization work about equally well on this example, though in general dropout seems to be the preferred method. They are both easy to add to a TF network. To drop out, say, 50% of the values coming out of the first layer of linear units (e.g., w1Out), we add to our program:

```
keepP= tf.placeholder(tf.float32)
w1Out=tf.nn.dropout(w1Out,keepP)
```

Note that we made the keep probability a placeholder. We typically want to do this because we do dropout only when training. When testing it is not needed, and indeed is harmful. By making the value a placeholder we can feed in the values 0.5 when we train and 1.0 when testing.

Using L2 regularization is just as easy. If we want to prevent the values of, e.g., W1, the weights of some linear units, from getting too large, we simply add:

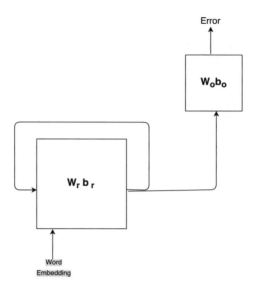

Figure 4.5: A graphical illustration of a recurrent NN

```
.01 * tf.nn.l2_loss(W1)
```

to the loss function we use when training. Here .01 is a hyperparameter
to weight how much we count the regularization compared to the original
cross-entropy loss. If your code computes perplexity by raising e to the per-
word loss, be sure to separate the combined loss used in training from the
loss used in the computation of perplexity. For the latter we only want the
cross-entropy loss.

4.5   Recurrent Networks

A *recurrent neural network* or *RNN* is, in some sense, the opposite of a
feed-forward NN. It is a network in which the output contributes to its own
input. In graph terminology it is a directed cyclic graph, as opposed to
feed-forward's directed acyclic graph. The simplest version of an RNN is
illustrated in Figure 4.5. The box labeled $\mathbf{W_r b_r}$ consists of a layer of linear
units with weights $\mathbf{W_r}$ and biases $\mathbf{b_r}$ plus an activation function. Input
comes into it from the bottom left and the output o goes out on the right
and splits. One copy circles back to itself; it is this circle that makes this
recurrent and not feed-forward. The other copy goes to a second layer of
linear units with parameters $\mathbf{W_o}, \mathbf{b_o}$ that is responsible for computing the

output of the RNN and the loss. Algebraically we can express this as follows:

$$s_0 = 0 \tag{4.8}$$

$$s_{t+1} = \rho((e_{t+1} \cdot s_t)W_r + b_r) \tag{4.9}$$

$$o = s_{t+1}W_o + b_o \tag{4.10}$$

We start the recurrence relation with the state s_0 initialized to some arbitrary value, typically a vector of zeros. The dimension of the state vector is a hyperparameter. We get the next state by concatenating the next input (e_{t+1}) with the previous state s_t, and feeding the result though the linear unit W_r, b_r. We then feed the output through the relu function ρ. (The choice of activation function is free.) Finally the output of the RNN unit o is obtained by feeding the current state through a second linear unit W_o, b_o. The training loss function is again a free choice, most commonly cross-entropy computed on o.

Recurrent networks are appropriate when we want previous inputs to the network to have an influence arbitrarily far into the future. Since language works this way, RNNs are frequently used in language-related tasks in general and language-modeling in particular. Thus here we assume the input is the embedding of the current word w_i, the prediction is w_{i+1} and the loss is our standard cross-entropy loss.

Computing the forward pass of the NN works pretty much as it does in a feed-forward NN except that we remember o from the previous iteration and concatenate it with the current word embedding at the start of the forward pass. The backward pass, however, is not so obvious. Earlier, in explaining how it is that the parameters in word embeddings are also updated by TF, we said TF works backward from the loss function, tracing back, continuing to look for parameters that have an effect on the error, and then differentiates the error with respect to those parameters. In Chapter 1's NN for Mnist this took us back through the layer with W and b, but then stopped when we encountered only the image pixels. The same is true for convolutional NNs, though the ways in which parameters enter into the error function computation are more complicated. But now there is potentially no limit on how far back we need go in the backward pass.

Suppose we read in the 500th word and want to change model parameters because we did not predict w_{501} with probability one. Tracing back, we find that part of the mistake is due to the weights W_o of the network in the upper right of Figure 4.5. But of course, one of the inputs to this layer is the output from the recurrent unit o_{500} from when it just processed word w_{500}. And where did this value come from? Well, W_r, b_r, but also in part

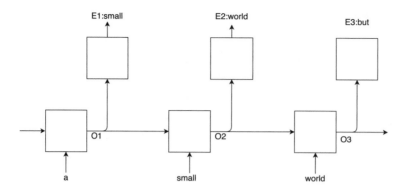

Figure 4.6: Back propagation through time with window size equal to three

it is due to o_{499}. To make a long story short, to do this "properly" we need to trace back the error through 500 loops of the recurrent layer, adjusting the weights $\mathbf{W_r}, \mathbf{b_r}$ over and over again due to the contributions from all the mistakes starting with word one. This is not practical.

We solve this problem by brute force. We simply cut off the computation after some arbitrary number of iterations backward. The number of iterations is called the *window size* and is a system hyperparameter. The overall technique is called *back propagation through time* and is illustrated in Figure 4.6, where we assume a window size of three. (A more realistic value for window size would be, say, twenty.) In more detail, Figure 4.6 imagines we are processing a corpus that starts with the phrase "It is a small world but I like it that way" along with sentence padding. Back propagation though time treats Figure 4.6 as if it were a feed-forward network taking in not a single word, but a window-size (i.e., three) of them and then computing the error on the three. For our short "corpus," the first call to training would take "STOP It is" as the input words and "it is a" as the three words to predict.

Figure 4.6 imagines we are on the second call, where the incoming words are "a small world" and they are to predict "small world but". At the start of the second forward pass the output from the first call comes in at the left (O0) and it is concatenated with the embedding of "a" and passed through the RNN to where it becomes O1 feeding the loss at E1.

But besides going to E1, O1 also goes on to be concatenated with the second word, "small". We compute the error there as well. Here we compute the effect of both $\mathbf{W}$ and $\mathbf{b}$ (not to mention embeddings) on the error in predicting "small". But $\mathbf{W}$ and $\mathbf{b}$ cause the error in two different ways —

STOP	It	is	a	small	world
but	I	like	it	that	way

STOP	It	is
but	I	like

a	small	world
it	that	way

Figure 4.7: Allotting words when batch size is two and window size is three

most directly from the error that leads from them to E2, but also from how they contributed to O1. Naturally when we next compute E3, **W** and **b** affect the error in three ways: directly from O3 from O1 and O2. So the parameters in those variables are modified six times (or, equivalently, the program keeps a running total and modifies them once).

Figure 4.6 ignores the issue of batch size. As you might expect, TF RNN functions are built to allow simultaneous batch-size training (and testing). So each call to the RNN takes a batch-size by window-size array of input to predict a similarly sized array of prediction words. As noted before, the semantics of this is that we are working on batch-size groups in parallel, so the last words predicted from the first training call are the first input words to the second.

To make this work out we need to be careful how we create the batches. Figure 4.7 illustrates what happens for the mock corpus "STOP It is a small world but l like it that way STOP". We assume a batch size of two and a window size of three. The basic idea is first to divide the corpus in two and then fill each batch from pieces from each part (in this case half) of the corpus. The top window in Figure 4.7 shows the corpus divided in two pieces. The next pair of windows shows the two input batches that are created from this. Each batch has three word segments from each half. We also need to batch up the prediction words to feed into the network. This is exactly like the above figure, but each word is one further along in the corpus. So the top line of the prediction diagram would read, "It is a small world but".

Since the "corpus" is 14 words, each half consists of six words. To see why six and not seven, concentrate on the predictions for the second batch. Go through carefully with seven words per half and you find that we do not have a prediction word for the last input. Thus the corpus is initially divided into S sections, where for a corpus of size x and a batch size b, $S = \lfloor (c-1)/b \rfloor$ (where "$\lfloor x \rfloor$" is the *floor function* — the largest integer smaller than x). Here the "minus one" gives the last input word its corresponding prediction word.

We have said nothing so far about what we do at the end of a sentence. The easiest thing is to simply plow on to the next. This means that a given window-size segment fed to the RNN can contain pieces of two different sentences. However, we have put the padding STOP word between them, so the RNN should, in principle, learn what that means in terms of what sorts of words are coming up — e.g., capitalized ones. Furthermore, there can be good clues about subsequent words from the last words of the previous sentence. If we are just concerned with language modeling, separating sentences with STOP but otherwise not worrying about sentence separation when training or using RNNs seems to be sufficient.

Let us review RNNs by looking again at Figures 4.5 and 4.6 and thinking about how we program the RNN language model. As we just noted, the code taking us from our word corpora to model input needs to be slightly revamped. Previously the input (and predictions) was a batch-size vector, now it is a batch-size by window-size array. We also need to turn each word into its word embedding, but this is unchanged from the feed-forward model.

Next, the word is fed into the RNN. The key TF code for the creation of the RNN is:

```
rnn= tf.contrib.rnn.BasicRNNCell(rnnSz)
initialState = rnn.zero_state(batchSz, tf.float32)
outputs, nextState = tf.nn.dynamic_rnn(rnn, embeddings,
                initial_state=initialState)
```

The first line here adds the RNN to the computation graph. Note that the width of the RNN's weight array is a free parameter, the `rnnSz` (you may remember that when we added an extra layer of linear units to the Mnist model at the end of Chapter 2 we had a similar situation). The last line is the call to the RNN. It takes three arguments, and returns two. The inputs are, first, the RNN proper, second, the words that the RNN is going to process (there are batch-size by window-size of them), and the `initialState` that it gets from the previous run. Since on the first call to `dynamic_rnn` there is no previous state, we create a dummy one with the function call on the second line `rnn.zero_state`.

`tf.nn.dynamic_rnn` has two outputs. The first, which we named `outputs`, is the information that feeds the error computation. In Figure 4.6 these are

```
[[-0.077   0.022  -0.058  -0.229   0.145]
 [-0.167   0.062   0.192  -0.310  -0.156]
 [-0.069  -0.050   0.203   0.000  -0.092]]

[[[-0.073  -0.121  -0.094  -0.213  -0.031]
  [-0.077   0.022  -0.058  -0.229   0.145]]
 [[ 0.179   0.099  -0.042  -0.012   0.175]
  [-0.167   0.062   0.192  -0.310  -0.156]]
 [[ 0.103   0.050   0.160  -0.141  -0.027]
  [-0.069  -0.050   0.203   0.000  -0.092]]]
```

Figure 4.8: `next_state` and `outputs` of an RNN

the outputs O1, O2, O3. So `output` has the shape [batch-size, window-size, hidden-size]. The first dimension packages up batch-size examples. Each example itself consists of O1, O2, and O3, so the second dimension is window-size. Last, e.g., O1 is a vector of rnn-size floats that comprise the RNN output from a single word.

The second output from `tf.nn.dynamic_rnn` we called `nextState` and it is the last output (O3) from this pass though the RNN. The next time we call `tf.nn.dynamic_rnn` we have `initialState = nextState`. Note that `nextState` is, in fact, information that is present in `outputs` since it is the collection of O3 from the batch-size examples. For example, Figure 4.8 shows `next_state` and `outputs` for batch-size three, window size two, and rnn size five. With window size two, every other line of the output is a next-state line. It is somewhat convenient to have the next state packaged up for us separately, but the real reason for this repetition will become clear in the next section.

The last piece of the language model is the loss. This is computed in the upper right-hand side of Figure 4.5. As we see there, the RNN output is first put through a layer of linear units to get the logits for softmax, and then we compute the cross-entropy loss from the probabilities. As just discussed, the output of the RNN is a 3D tensor with shape [batch-size, window-size, rnn-size]. Up until now we have only passed 2D tensors, matrices, through our linear units, and we have done so with matrix multiplication — e.g., `tf.matmul(inpt, W)`.

The easiest way to handle this is to change the shape of the RNN output tensor to make it a matrix with the correct properties:

```
output2 = tf.reshape(output,[batchSz*windowSz, rnnSz])
logits = matmul(output2,W)
```

Here **W** is the linear layer (**W$_o$**) that takes the output of the RNN and turns it into the logits in Figure 4.5. We then can hand this to `tf.nn.sparse_softmax_cross_entropy_with_logits`, which returns a column vector of loss values that reduce to a single value with `tf.reduce_mean`. This final value can be exponentiated to give us our perplexity.

Changing the shape of the RNN output was convenient here for pedagogical reasons (it allowed us to reuse `tf.matmul`) and computational ones (it put things into the shape required by **sparse_softmax**). In other situations the downstream computation might require the original shape. For this we can turn to one of many TF functions that handle multidimensional tensors. Here the one we would use is that covered in Section 2.4.2. The call to it would be:

```
tf.tensordot(outputs, W, [[2], [0]])
```

This code performs a repeated dot product (in effect, a matrix multiplication) between the second component (zero-based) of `outputs` and the zeroth of `W`.

One more point about the use of general RNN. In the Python code that goes along with the above TF code for RNNs we see something like this:

```
inputSt = sess.run(initialSt)
for i in range(numExamps)
    ''read in words and embed them''
    logts, nxts=sess.run([logits,nextState],
                        {{input=wrds, nextState=inputSt})
    inputSt=nxts
```

Nothing here should be taken literally except (a) how the input state for the RNN is initialized, (b) how we pass it to TF with the piece of the feed dictionary `nextState=inputState`, and (c) how we then update `inputSt` in the last line above. Up until now we have only used **feed_dict** to pass values to TF placeholders. Here `nextState` points not to a placeholder, but rather a piece of code that generates the zero state with which we start the RNN. This is allowed.

4.6   Long Short-Term Memory

A *long short-term memory* NN (*LSTM*) is a particular kind of RNN that almost always outperforms the simple RNN presented in the last section.

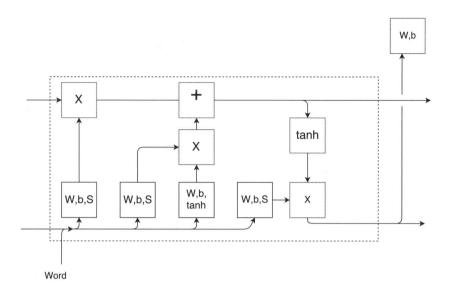

Figure 4.9: The architecture of LSTMs

The problem with standard RNNs is that while the goal is to remember things from far back, in practice they seem to forget quickly. In Figure 4.9 everything in the dotted box corresponds to a single RNN unit. Obviously LSTMs elaborate the architecture quite significantly. First, note that we have shown one copy of an LSTM in a back-prop-though-time diagram. So on the left we have information coming in from processing the previous word (using two tensors of information rather than one). At the bottom we have the next word coming in. On the right we have two tensors going out to inform the next time unit and, as in plain RNNs, we have this information going "up" in the diagram to predict the next word and the loss (upper right-hand side).

The goal is to improve the RNN's memory of past events by training it to remember the important stuff and forget the rest. To this end, LSTMs pass two versions of the past. The "official" selective memory is at the top and a more local version at the bottom. The top memory timeline is called the *cell state* and abbreviated c. The lower line is called h.

Figure 4.9 introduces several new connectives and activation functions. First, we see that the memory line is modified at two locations before being passed on to the next time unit. They are labeled times (X), and plus (+). The idea is that memories are removed at the times unit, and added at the plus unit.

Why do we say this? Look now at the current word embedding coming in at the bottom left. It goes through a layer of linear units followed by a sigmoid activation function, as indicated by the $\mathbf{W}, \mathbf{b}, \mathbf{S}$ annotation: $\mathbf{W}, \mathbf{b}$ make up the linear unit and $\mathbf{S}$ is the sigmoid function. We showed the sigmoid function in Figure 2.7. You might want to review it because a few of its specifics matter in the following discussion. In math notation we have the operation:

$$\mathbf{h'} \;=\; \mathbf{h_t} \cdot \mathbf{e} \tag{4.11}$$

$$\mathbf{f} \;=\; S((\mathbf{h'W_f} + \mathbf{b_f}) \tag{4.12}$$

We use a center dot $\cdot$ to indicate concatenation of vectors. To repeat, at lower left we concatenate the previous h-line $\mathbf{h_t}$ and the current word embedding $\mathbf{e}$ to give h', which in turn is fed into the "forgetting" linear unit (followed by a sigmoid) to produce $\mathbf{f}$, the forgetting signal that is moving up the left-hand side of the figure.

The output of the sigmoid is then multiplied element-wise with the memory c-line coming in top left. (By "element-wise" we mean that, e.g., the $x[i, j]$th element of one array is multiplied by (or added to, etc.) the $y[i, j]$th the element of the other.)

$$\mathbf{c'_t} = \mathbf{c_t} \odot \mathbf{f} \tag{4.13}$$

(Here "$\odot$" indicates element-wise multiplication.) Given that sigmoids are bounded by zero and one, the result of the multiplication must be a reduction in the absolute value at each point of the main memory. This corresponds to "forgetting." Overall this configuration, sigmoid feeding a multiplicative layer, is a common pattern when we want "soft" gating.

Contrast this with the goings on at the additive unit that the memory next encounters. Again, the next word embedding has come in from bottom left, and this time it goes separately through two linear layers, one with sigmoid activation, one with the *tanh activation function*, shown in Figure 4.10. Tanh stands for *hyperbolic tangent*.

$$\mathbf{a_1} \;=\; S(\mathbf{h'W_{a_1}} + \mathbf{b_{a_1}}) \tag{4.14}$$

$$\mathbf{a_2} \;=\; \tanh((\mathbf{h_t} \cdot \mathbf{e})\mathbf{W_{a_2}} + \mathbf{b_{a_2}}) \tag{4.15}$$

It is important that, unlike the sigmoid function, tanh can output both positive and negative values, so it can express new material as opposed to just scale. The result of this is added to the cell state at the cell labeled "+":

$$\mathbf{c_{t+1}} = \mathbf{c'_t} \oplus (\mathbf{a_1} \odot \mathbf{a_2}) \tag{4.16}$$

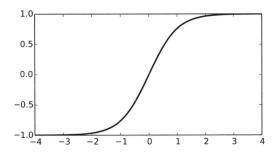

Figure 4.10: The tanh function

After this the cell memory line splits. One copy goes out the right, and one copy goes through a tanh and is then combined with a linear transformation of the more local history/embedding to become the new h-line on the bottom:

$$\mathbf{h}'' = \mathbf{h}'\mathbf{W_h} + b_h \tag{4.17}$$

$$\mathbf{h_{t+1}} = \mathbf{h}'' \odot a_2 \tag{4.18}$$

This is to be concatenated with the next word embedding, and the process repeats. The point to be emphasized here is that the cell-memory line never goes directly though linear units. Things are de-emphasized (e.g., forgotten) at the "X" unit and added at "+," but that is it. Thus the logic of the LSTM mechanism.

As for the program, only one small change is needed to the TF version:

```
tf.contrib.rnn.BasicRNNCell(rnnSz)
```

becomes

```
tf.contrib.rnn.LSTMCell(rnnSz)
```

Note that this change affects the state that is passed from one time unit to the next. Previously, as shown in Figure 4.8, the states had shape [batchSz, rnnSz]. Now it is [2, batchSz, rnnSz], one [batchSz, rnnSz] tensor for the c-line, one for the h-line.

In performance the LSTM version is much better, at the cost of taking longer to train. Take an RNN model such as that we developed in the last section, give it plenty of resources (word-embedding vectors of size 128, hidden size of 512) and we get a respectable perplexity of 120 or so. Make the single function call change from an RNN to a LSTM and our perplexity goes down to 101.

4.7   References and Further Readings

The paper that introduced what we now think of as the standard feed-forward language model is that by Bengio et al. [BDVJ03]. It also originated the term "word embedding." The idea of representing words in a continuous space, particularly vectors of numbers, is much earlier. It is the Bengio paper, however, that showed that word embeddings as we now know them are almost automatic byproducts of NN language models.

Arguably, it is not until the work of Mikolov et al. that word embeddings became a near universal component of NN natural-language processing. They developed several models that go by the name of *word2vec*. The standard paper is [MSC+13]. The most popular of the word2vec models is *skip-gram model*. In our presentation, embeddings were optimized to predict the next word given the previous words. In the skip-gram model each single word is asked to predict all its neighboring words. One striking result of the word2vec models is the use of word embeddings to solve *word analogy problems* — e.g., Male is to king as female is to what? Unexpectedly, answers to these problems fell out from the word embeddings they created. One simply took the embedding for the word "king", subtracted that for "male", added "female", and then looked for the word embedding nearest the result. A great blog on word embeddings and their issues is that by Sebastian Ruder [Rud16].

Recurrent neural networks have been around since at least the mid-1980s, but they did not perform well until Sepp Hochreiter and Jürgen Schmidhuber created LSTMs [HS97]. A blog by Chris Colah gives a good explanation of LSTMs [Col15], and my Figure 4.9 is a reworking of one of his diagrams.

4.8   Written Exercises

Exercise 4.1: Assume that our corpus starts out " *STOP* I like my cat and my cat likes me . *STOP*" . Also assume that we assign individual words their unique integer as we read in the corpus, starting with 0. If we have batch size 5, write out the values we should read in to fill the placeholders `inpu` and `answr` on the first training batch.

Exercise 4.2: Explain why, if you hope to have any chance of learning a good embedding-based language model, you may not set all of **E** to zero. Make sure your explanation also works for setting all of **E** to one.

Exercise 4.3: Explain why, if you are using L2 regularization, it is positively a bad idea to compute the actual total loss.

Exercise 4.4: Consider building a trigram-fully-connected language model. In our version we concatenated the embeddings for the two previous inputs to form the model input. Does the order in which we concatenate have any effect on the model's ability to learn? Explain.

Exercise 4.5: Consider an NN unigram model. Can its model perplexity be any better than picking words from a uniform distribution? Why or why not? Explain what pieces of the bigram model are needed for optimal performance of a unigram model.

Exercise 4.6: A *linear gated unit* (LGU) is a variant of LSTMs. Referring back to Figure 4.9, we see that the latter has one hidden layer that controls what gets removed from the main memory line, and a second that controls what is added. In both cases the layers take the lower line of control as input, and produce a vector of numbers between 0 and 1 that are multiplied with the memory line (forgetting) or added to it (remembering). LGUs differ in replacing these two layers by a single layer with the same input. The output is multiplied by the control line as before. However, it is also subtracted from one, multiplied by the control layer, and added to the memory line. In general, LGUs work as well as LSTMs and, having one fewer linear layer, are slightly faster. Explain the intuition. Modify Figure 4.9 so it represents the workings of a LGU.

Chapter 5

Sequence-to-Sequence Learning

Sequence-to-sequence learning (typically abbreviated *seq2seq*) is a deep learning technique for mapping a sequence of symbols to another sequence of symbols when it is not possible (or at least we cannot see how) to perform the mapping on the basis of the individual symbols themselves. The prototypical application for seq2seq is *machine translation* (abbreviated *MT*) — having a computer translate between natural languages such as French and English.

It has been recognized since around 1990 that expressing this mapping in a program is quite difficult, and that a more indirect approach works much better. We give the computer an *aligned corpus* — many examples of sentence pairs that are mutual translations of each other — and require the machine to figure out the mapping for itself. This is where deep learning comes in. Unfortunately, the deep learning-techniques we have learned for natural-language tasks, e.g., LSTMs, by themselves are not sufficient for MT.

Critically, language modeling, the task we concentrated on in the last chapter, proceeds on a word-by-word basis. That is, we put in a word and we predict the next one. MT does not work like this. Consider some examples from the *Canadian Hansard's*, the record of everything that has been said in the Canadian parliament that by law must be published in Canada's two official languages, French and English. The first pair of sentences of a section I happen to have at hand is:

> edited hansard number 1
> hansard révisé numéro 1

An early lesson for English speakers learning French (and presumably vice versa) is that adjectives typically go before the noun they modify in English, and after in French. So here the adjectives "edited" and "révisé" are not in the same positions in the translations. The point is that we cannot work our way left to right in the *source language* (the language we are translating from) spitting out one word at a time in the *target language*. In this case we could have input two words and output two, but the observed sequential mismatches can grow much larger. The following occurs a few lines after the previous example. Note that the text is tokenized — twice the French punctuation is separated from the words to which it would ordinarily be attached:

> this being the day on which parliament was convoked by proclamation of his excellency ...
>
> parlement ayant été convoqué pour aujourd ' hui , par proclamation de son excellence ...

The word-by-word translation of the French would be "parliament having been convoked for today, by proclamation of his excellency," and in particular "this being the day" is translated into "aujourd ' hui." (Indeed, generally the lengths of the sentences in the pair are not the same.) Thus the requirement for sequence-to-sequence learning, where a sequence is generally taken to be a complete sentence.

5.1   The Seq2Seq Paradigm

The diagram of a very simple seq2seq model is shown in Figure 5.1. It shows the process over time (time as usual running from left to right) of translating "hansard révisé numero 1" into "edited hansard number 1". The model consists of two RNNs. As opposed to LSTMs, we are assuming an RNN model that passes a single memory line. We could use `BasicRNNCell`; however, a better choice is a newer competitor to the LSTM, the *Gated Recurrent Unit*, or *GRU*, which passes only a single memory line between time units.

The model operates in two passes, each having its own GRU. The first pass is called the *encoding pass* and is represented in the lower half of Figure 5.1. The pass ends when the last French token (always STOP) is processed by the lower GRU. The GRU state is then passed on to the second half of the process. The goal of this pass is to produce a vector that "summarizes" the sentence. This is sometimes called a *sentence embedding* by analogy to word embeddings.

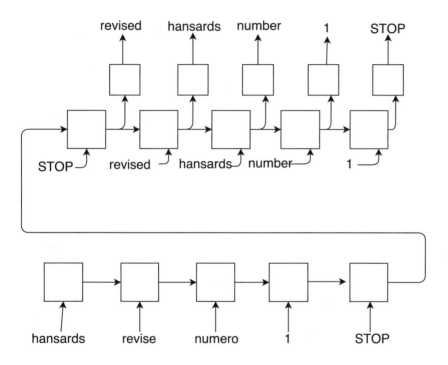

Figure 5.1: A simple sequence-to-sequence learning model

The second half of seq2seq learning is called the *decoding pass*. As seen in the figure, it is a pass through the target language (here English) sentence. (Perhaps it is time to make explicit that we are talking here about what happens during training, so we know the English sentence.) This time the goal is to predict the next English word after each word is input. The loss function is the usual cross-entropy loss.

The terms *encode* and *decode* come from communication theory. A message must be encoded to form the signal that is sent, and then decoded back again from the signal that is received. If there is noise in the communication the signal received will not necessarily be identical to the one sent. Imagine that the original message was English and the noise converted it to French. Then the process of translating it (back) to English is "decoding."

Note that the first input word for the decoding pass is the padding word STOP. It is also the last word to be output. Were we to use the model for real French-to-English MT, the system does not have the English available. But it can assume that we start the processing with STOP. Then to generate each subsequent word we give the LSTM the previous predicted word. It stops processing when the LSTM predicts that the next "word" should be STOP again. Naturally we should also work this way when testing. Then we know the English, but we only use that information for evaluation. This means that in actual translation we predict the next translation word partly on the basis of the last translated word, *which could very well be a mistake.* If it is, then there is greatly increased likelihood that the next word will be wrong, etc.

In this chapter we ignore the complexity of real MT by evaluating our program's ability to predict the correct next English word given the correct previous word. Of course in real MT there is no single correct English translation for a particular French sentence, so just because our program does not predict the exact word used in our parallel corpus' translation does not mean it is wrong. Objective MT evaluation is a topic of importance, but one we ignore here.

One last simplification before we look at writing an NN MT program. Figure 5.1 is laid out as a back-propagation-though-time diagram, so all the RNN units in the bottom row are actually the same recurrent unit, but at successive times. Similarly for the units in the top row. As you may remember, back-prop-though-time models have a window-size hyperparameter. In MT we want to process an entire sentence in one fell swoop, but sentences come in all sizes. (In the Penn Treebank they range from one word to over 150.) We simplify our program by working only on sentences where both the French and English are less than 12 words long, or 13 including a STOP

```
1  with tf.variable_scope("enc"):
2    F = tf.Variable(tf.random_normal((vfSz,embedSz),stddev=.1))
3    embs = tf.nn.embedding_lookup(F, encIn)
4    embs = tf.nn.dropout(embs, keepPrb)
5    cell = tf.contrib.rnn.GRUCell(rnnSz)
6    initState = cell.zero_state(bSz, tf.float32)
7    encOut, encState = tf.nn.dynamic_rnn(cell, embs,
8                                       initial_state=initState)
9
10 with tf.variable_scope("dec"):
11   E = tf.Variable(tf.random_normal((veSz,embedSz),stddev=.1))
12   embs = tf.nn.embedding_lookup(E, decIn)
13   embs = tf.nn.dropout(embs, keepPrb)
14   cell = tf.contrib.rnn.GRUCell(rnnSz)
15   decOut,_ = tf.nn.dynamic_rnn(cell, embs, initial_state=encState)
```

Figure 5.2: TF for two RNNs in an MT model

word. We then make each sentence length 13 by adding extra padding STOPs. Thus the program can assume that all sentences have the same length of 13 words. So consider the short French-English aligned sentences with which we started our discussion of MT, "edited hansard number 1" and "hansard révisé numéro 1". The French sentence we input would look like this:

> hansard révisé numéro 1 STOP STOP STOP STOP STOP STOP STOP STOP STOP

and the English:

> STOP edited hansard number 1 STOP STOP STOP STOP STOP STOP STOP STOP STOP

5.2 Writing a Seq2Seq MT program

Let us start by reviewing the RNN models we covered in Chapter 4, with a slight twist. So far we have not paid much attention to good software engineering practices. Here, however, TF, for reasons to be explained, forces us to clean up our act. Since we are creating two nearly identical RNN models we introduce the TF construct variable_scope. Figure 5.2 shows the TF code for the two RNNs we need in our simple seq2seq model.

```
W = tf.Variable(tf.random_normal([rnnSz,veSz],stddev=.1))
b = tf.Variable(tf.random_normal([veSz,stddev=.1))
logits = tf.tensordot(decOut,W,axes=[[2],[0]])+b
loss = tf.contrib.seq2seq.sequence_loss(logits, ans,
                                        tf.ones([bSz, wSz]))
```

Figure 5.3: TF for seq2seq decoder

We divide the code into two pieces; the first creates the encoding RNN, and the second the decoding. Each section is enclosed within a TF `variable_scope` command. This function takes one argument, a string to serve as the name for the scope. The purpose of `variable_scope` is to let us package together a group of commands in such a way as to avoid variable-name conflicts. For, example, both the top and bottom segments use the variable name `cell` in such a way that without two separate scopes, they would have stepped on each other with very bad results.

But even if we had been careful and given each of our variables unique names, this code *still* would not have worked correctly. For reasons buried in TF code details, when `dynamic_rnn` creates the material to insert into the TF graph, it always uses the same name to point to it. Unless we put the two calls in separate scopes (or unless the code is set up not to mind that the two calls are, in fact, one and the same), we get an error message.

Now consider the code within each variable scope. For the encoder we first create space for the French-word embeddings, `F`. We assume a placeholder named `encIn` that accepts a tensor of French-word indices with shape batch size by window size. The lookup function then returns a 3D tensor, of shape batch size by window size by embedding size (line 3), to which we apply dropout with the probability of keeping a connection set to `keepProb` (line 4). We then create the RNN cell, this time using the GRU variant of the LSTM. Line 7 then uses the cell to produce the outputs and the next state.

The second GRU is parallel to the first, except that the call to `dynamic_rnn` takes as its input the state output of the encoder RNN, rather than a zero-valued initial state. This is the `state=encState` in line 15. Again consulting Figure 5.1, the decoder RNN's word-by-word output feeds into a linear layer. The figure does not show, but the reader should imagine, the layer's output (the logits) feeding into a loss computation. The code would look like that in Figure 5.3. The only thing new here is the call to `seq2seq_loss`, a specialized version of cross-entropy loss in cases when logits are 3D tensors. It

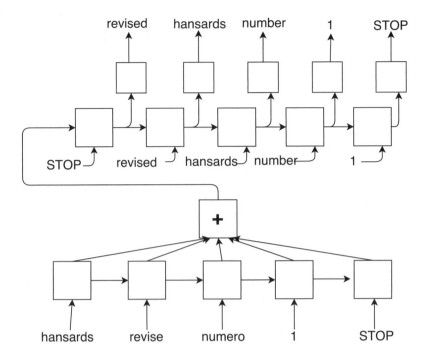

Figure 5.4: Seq2seq sentence summarization by addition

takes three arguments, the first two standard — the logits and a 2D tensor of correct answer (batch size by window size). The third argument allows a weighted sum — for situations where some errors should count more toward the total loss than others. In our case we want every mistake to count equally, so the third argument has all weights equal to 1.

As we said earlier, the whole idea of the simplest seq2seq model in Figure 5.1 is that the encoding pass creates a "summary" of the French sentence by passing the French though the GRU and then using the final GRU state output as the summary. There are, however, a lot of different ways to create such sentence summaries, and a significant body of research has been devoted to looking at these alternatives. Figure 5.4 shows a second model that for MT is slightly superior. The difference in implementation is small: rather than pass the encoder final state to the decoder as its start state, we rather take the sum of all the encoder states. Since we padded all the French and English sentences to be of length 13, this means that we take all 13 states and sum them. The hope is that this sum is more informative than the one final vector, which in fact seems to be the case.

Actually, your author chose to take the mean of the state vectors as opposed to the sum. If you go back to chapter 1 and look at the forward pass computation, you will remember that taking the mean rather than the sum makes no difference in the final probabilities, as softmax will wash any multiplicative differences away, and taking the mean just corresponds to dividing by window size (13). Furthermore, the direction of the parameter gradient does not change either. What can and does change is the magnitude of the change we make in the parameter values. In the current situation taking the sum is roughly equivalent to multiplying the learning rate by 13. As a general practice it is better in such situations to keep parameter values near zero, and modify the learning rate directly.

5.3   Attention in Seq2seq

The notion of *attention* in seq2seq models arises from the idea that, although in general we need to understand an entire sentence before we can translate it, in practice for a given patch of target word translations, some parts of the source sentence are more important than others. In particular, much more often than not, the first few French words inform the first few English, the middle of the French sentence leads to the middle of the English, etc. While this is particularly true for English and French, which are very similar as languages go, even languages which have no obvious commonalities have this property. The reason is the *given new distinction*. It seems to be the case in all languages that, when saying something new about things we have already been talking about (and this is usually what happens in coherent conversation or writing), we first mention the "given" — what we have been talking about, and only then mention the new material. So in a conversation about Jack we might say, "Jack ate a cookie," but if we were talking about a batch of cookies, "One of the cookies was eaten by Jack."

Figure 5.5 illustrates a small variation on the summing seq2seq mechanism of Figure 5.4 in which the summary concatenated with the English word embedding is fed into the decoder cell at each window position. This contrasts with Figure 5.4, where just the English word is fed in. From our new viewpoint, this model gives equal attention to all the states from the encoder when working on all parts of the English. In attention models we modify this so that different states are mixed together in different proportions before being handed to the decoder RNN. We call this *position-only attention*. True attention models are more complicated, but we leave this to Further Reading.

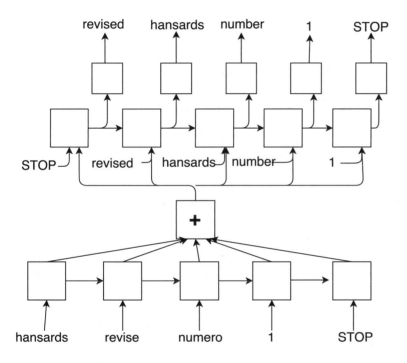

Figure 5.5: Seq2seq where the encoder summary is fed directly to each decoder window position

$$\begin{array}{ccc} 1/2 & 1/6 & 1/6 \\ 1/6 & 1/3 & 1/6 \\ 1/6 & 1/3 & 1/3 \\ 1/6 & 1/6 & 1/3 \end{array}$$

Figure 5.6: A possible weight matrix for weighting corresponding French/English positions more highly

So we are going to build an attention scheme where, say, the attention an English word at position i pays to the state of the French encoding at position j depends only on i and j. Generally, the closer i and j, the greater the attention. Figure 5.6 gives an imaginary weight matrix for a model in which the encoder (French) window size is 4 and the decoder size is 3. Heretofore we have assumed both window sizes to be 13, but there is no reason they have to be the same. Furthermore, since French has about 10% more words than a corresponding English translation, there is good reason to pair slightly larger French window sizes with smaller English ones. In addition, for pedagogical reasons, making the matrix asymmetrical helps keep straight which numbers are refering to English word positions and which are talking about French.

Here we assign $W[i, j]$ to be the weight given to the ith French state when used to predict the jth English word. So the total weight for any English word is the column sum, which we have made 1. E.g., the first column gives the weights for the first English word. Looking at the first column, we see that the first French state counts for half of the emphasis (in our imagined window size of 4), and the remaining three French states all share the remaining emphasis equally. For the moment we assume that in our real program a $13 * 13$ version of Figure 5.6 is a TF constant.

Next, given the $13 * 13$ weight matrix, how do we use it to vary the attention for a particular English output? Figure 5.7 shows the tensor flow and sample numerical calculations for the situation where batch size is 2, window size 3, and RNN size is 4. At the top we see an imaginary encoder output encOut. The batch size is 2, and to make things simple we made the two batches identical. Within each batch we have the three vectors of length 4, each being the length 4 (RNN size) vector for the RNN output at that window position. So, for example, in batch 0, the first (0-based) state vector is (1, 1, 1, 1).

Next we have our made-up weight vector, wAT, of dimensions $4 * 3$ (the window sizes). It is French state position by English word position. So

```
eo=  ( ((  1, 2, 3, 4),
        (  1, 1, 1, 1),
        (  1, 1, 1, 1),
        ( -1, 0,-1, 0)),
       ((  1, 2, 3, 4),
        (  1, 1, 1, 1),
        (  1, 1, 1, 1),
        ( -1, 0,-1, 0)) )
encOut=tf.constant(eo, tf.float32)

AT = (  ( .6, .25, .25 ),
        ( .2, .25, .25 ),
        ( .1, .25, .25 ),
        ( .1, .25, .25 )  )
wAT = tf.constant(AT, tf.float32)

encAT = tf.tensordot(encOut,wAT,[[1],[0]])
sess= tf.Session()

print sess.run(encAT)
'''[[[ 0.80000001  0.5         0.5         ]
    [ 1.50000012  1.          1.          ]
    [ 2.          1.          1.          ]
    [ 2.70000005  1.5         1.5         ]]
    ...] '''

decAT = tf.transpose(encAT,[0, 2, 1])
print sess.run(decAT)
'''[[[ 0.80000001  1.50000012  2.          2.70000005]
    [ 0.5         1.          1.          1.5        ]
    [ 0.5         1.          1.          1.5        ]]
    ...]'''
```

Figure 5.7: Simplified attention calculations with bSz = 2, wSz = 3, and rnnSz = 4

the first column says, in effect, that the first English word should be given a state vector that is 60% the first French state vector and 20% each of the other two RNN state vectors. It is arranged so that the weights for each English word add up to 100%.

Next come the three TF commands that allow us to take in the unweighted encoder states and produce the weighted versions for each English word decision. First we rearrange the encoder output tensor, from [bSz, wSz, rnnSz] to [bSz, rnnSz, wSz]. This is done by the tf.transpose command. The transpose command takes two arguments, the tensor to be transposed and a bracketed vector of integers specifying the transpose to be performed. Here we asked for [0, 2, 1] — keep the 0th dimension in place, but the "2" says to make the dimension that was originally the second become dimension 1, and the final 1 makes the last dimension what used to be the first. We show the result of this transform where we executed print sess.run(encOT),

We effected the transposition to make it easy to do the matrix multiplication in the next step (the tensordot). In fact, if we do not have the complication of batch size, we are multiplying tensors of shape [rnnSz, wSz] * [wSz,wSz], and we could use standard matrix multiplication (matmul). The extra dimension induced by batch size nixes this possibility and we fall back on

```
encAT = tf.tensordot)(encOut.wAT,[[1],[0]])
```

Last we reverse the transposition we did two steps ago to put the encoder output states back into their original form.

It is worth pausing a bit to compare the final result at the bottom of Figure 5.7 with our imaginary encoder output at the top of the figure. The column (.6, .2, .2) says to hand the first English word a vector composed of 60% "state" zero, which is [1, 2, 3, 4]. So we expect the resulting state to increase as we go from left to right, which (.6, 1.4, 1.8, 2.6) does. The second state, of all 1s, does not have much effect (it adds .2 to each position). But the last state (0, −1, 0. −1) should make the the result have an up-and-down pattern, which it does, sort of. (They components of (.6, 1.4, 1.8, 2.6) all increase, but the first and third increases are larger than the second.)

Once we have the reweighted encoder states to feed the decoder, we concatenate each with the English word embedding that we were already feeding into the decoder RNN. This completes our simple attention MT system. However, one thing is important to finish this example: we can trivially have our program learn the attention weights by just making our $13 * 13$ attention array a TF variable rather than a constant. The idea

−6.3	**1.3**	.37	.13	.06	.04	.11	.10	.02
−.66	−..44	**.64**	.26	.16	.02	.03	.04	.06
−.38	−.47	−.04	**.63**	.18	.10	.07	.06	.12
−.30	−.44	−.35	−.15	**.48**	.24	.06	.13	0
−.02	−.16	−.35	−.37	−.23	.12	**.32**	.22	11
.05	−.11	−.11	−.35	−04	−.22	.05	**.26**	.24
.10	.02	−.04	−.23	−.32	−33	−.25	−.01	**.28**
0	.03	.01	−.18	−.21	−.26	−.30	−.1.1	−.17

Figure 5.8: Attention weights for the $8 * 9$ top left corner of the $13 * 13$ attention weight matrix

is similar to what we did when in Chapter 3 we had the NN learning the convolution kernels. Figure 5.8 shows some of the weights learned in this fashion. The bold numbers are the highest numbers in their row. They show the expected rightward shift — the translation of words in the beginning, middle, or end of the English should, in general, pay most attention to the beginning, middle, or end of the French.

5.4 Multilength Seq2Seq

In the last section we restricted our translation pairs to examples where both sentences are 12 words or less (13 including a STOP padding). In real MT such limitations would not be permitted. On the other hand, having a window of, say, 65, which would allow the translation of virtually all sentences that came our way, would mean that a more normal sentence would end up padded with 40 or 50 STOPs. The solution that has been adopted in the NN MT community is to create models with multiple window lengths. We now show how this works.

Consider again lines 5–8 of Figure 5.2. From our current perspective, it is striking that neither of the two TF commands primarily responsible for setting up the encoder RNN mentions the window size. GRU creation needs to know the RNN size since, after all, it is in charge of allocating space for the GRU's variables. But window size does not enter into this activity. On the other hand, `dynamic_rnn` certainly *does* need to know the window size, since it is responsible for creating the pieces of the TF graphic that execute back propagation through time. And it gets the information, in this case by way of the variable `embds`, which is of size `[bSz, wSz, embedSz]`. So suppose we decide to support two different window-size combinations. The first, say, handles all sentences where the French is 14 words or less and the English 12 words or less. The second we make double this, 28 and 24. If either the French is larger than 28 or the English larger than 24 we throw out the example. If either the French or English is larger than 14 or 12, respectively, but smaller than the 28, 24 limits, we put the pair into the larger group. We then create one GRU to use in both `dynamic_rnns` as follows:

```
cell = tf.contrib.rnn.GRUCell(rnnSz)
encOutSmall, encStateS = tf.nn.dynamic_rnn(cell, smallerEmbs, ...)
encOutLarge, encStateL= tf.nn.dynamic_rnn(cell, largerEmbs, ...)
```

Note that while we have two (or potentially five or six) `dynamnic_rnns`, depending on the range of sizes we want to accommodate, they all share the same GRU cell so they learn and share the same knowledge of French. In a similar fashion we would create one English GRU cell, etc.

5.5   Programming Exercise

This chapter has concentrated on NN technology used in MT, so here we endeavor to built a translation program. Unfortunately, in the current state of deep learning this is very difficult. While recent progress has been impressive, the programs that boast good results require about a billion training examples and days of training, if not longer. This does not make for a good student assignment.

Instead we will use about a million training examples — some of the Canadian Hansard's text restricted to French/English training examples where both sentences are 12 words or less (13 including the STOP padding). We also set our hyperparameters on the small side: embedding size of 30, RNN size of 64, and we only train for one epoch. We set the learning rate to .005.

As noted earlier, evaluating MT programs is difficult, short of going through and grading its translations by hand. We adopt a particularly simple-minded scheme. We go through the correct English translation until we hit the first STOP. A machine-generated word is considered correct if the word in the same position in the Hansard's English is identical. To repeat, we stop scoring after the first STOP. For example,

the	law	is	very	clear	.	STOP
the	*UNK*	is	a	clear	.	STOP

would count as 5 correct out of 7 words. At the end we divide the total number of correct words by the total of all words in the development set English sentences.

With this metric your author's implementation scored 59% correct on the test set after one epoch (65% after the second, and 67% after three). Whether this sounds good or bad depends on your prior expectations. Given our earlier comments about needing a billion training examples, perhaps your expectations were low; certainly ours were. However, an examination of the translations produced shows that even 59% is misleadingly optimistic. We ran the program printing out the first sentence in every 400th batch using a batch size of 32. The first two training examples of inputs correctly translated were:

```
Epoch 0 Batch 6401 Cor: 0.432627
* * *
* * *
* * *


Epoch 0 Batch 6801 Cor: 0.438996
le très hon. jean chrétien
right hon. jean chrétien
right hon. jean chrétien
```

Here "* * *" is inserted between sessions of parliament by the editor. 14,410 lines of the file of 351,846 lines consist solely of this marking. By this point in the first epoch (it is halfway through) the program has no doubt memorized the corresponding "English" (which is, of course, identical). In a similar vein, the names of the next speaker are always added to the Hansard's before what they say. Jean Chrétien was the prime minister of Canada during this volume of the Hansard's, and he seems to have spoken 64 times. So the translation of this French sentence was also memorized. Indeed, one might ask if any of the correct translations are *not* memorized. The answer is yes, but not that many. Here are the last six from the 22,000 example test set.

```
19154 the problem is very serious .
21191 hon. george s. baker :
21404 mr. bernard bigras ( rosemont , bq ) moved :
21437 mr. bernard bigras ( rosemont , bq ) moved :
21741 he is correct .
21744 we will support the bill .
```

These are from a run with double attention for corresponding words, a RNN size of 64, learning rate of .005, and one epoch. The accuracy metric described earlier was 68.6% for the test set. We printed out any test example that was completely correct and did not correspond to any English training sentence.

It is interesting and useful to get some idea of how the state changes between words of a sentence. In particular, the first seq2seq model used the encoder final state to prime the English decoder. Since we just took the state at word 13, no matter the length of the original French (maximum 12 words), we are assuming that we have not lost much by taking the state after, say, eight STOPs if the original French were five words. To test this, we looked at the 13 states produced by the encoder and for each state computed the cosine similarity between successive states. The following is from a training sentence being processed in the third epoch:

> English: that has already been dealt with .
> Translation: it is a . a . .
> French word indices:[18, 528, 65, 6476, 41, 0, 0, 0, 0, 0, 0, 0, 0]
> State similarity: .078 .57 .77 .70 .90 1 1 1 1 1 1 1 1

You might first notice the terrible quality of the "translation" (two words correct out of 8, ".", and STOP). The state similarities, however, look reasonable. In particular, once we hit the end of the sentence at word f5 (in the French), all the state similarities are 1.0 — so the state does not change at all due to the padding, as we hoped.

The least similar states are the first compared to the second. From there the similarity increases almost monotonically. Or in other words, as we progress through the sentence there is more past information worth preserving, so more of the old state hangs around, making the next state similar to the current one.

5.6   Written Exercises

Exercise 5.1: Suppose we are using multiple-length seq2seq for an MT program and have decided on two sentence sizes, one for up to 7 words (and STOPs) for English and 10 for French and the other for up to 10 words for English and 13 for French. Write out the input if the French sentence is "A B C D E F" and the English is "M N O P Q R S T".

Exercise 5.2: We chose to illustrate attention in Section 5.3 with a particularly simple form, one that based the attention decision only on the location of the attention in both the French and English. A more sophisticated version bases the decision on the input state vectors to the English position we are working on and the proposed state vector whose influence we are deciding. While this can allow more sophisticated judgments, it requires a significant complication of the model. In particular, we can no longer use standard TF recurrent network back propagation through time for the decoder. Explain why.

Exercise 5.3: It has frequently been observed that feeding the source language into the seq2seq encoder *backward* (but leaving the decoder working forward) improves MT performance by a slight but constant amount. Make up a plausible story for why this could be the case.

Exercise 5.4: In principle, we could have a seq2seq model with two losses that we add together to make the total loss. One would be the current MT loss incurred by not predicting the next target word with probability 1. The second could be a loss in the encoder, asking the encoder to predict the next source (e.g., French) word — i.e., a language model loss. (a) Make up a plausible story for why this will degrade performance. (b) Make up a plausible story for why this will improve performance.

5.7 References and Further Readings

In the 1980s a group at IBM led by Fred Jelinek began work on a project to create a machine translation program by having the machine learn to translate by noticing statistical regularities. The "noticing" came from Bayesian machine learning and the data, as in this chapter, came from the Canadian Hansard's corpus [BCP+88]. This approach, after a few years of ridicule, became the dominant approach, and remained so until recently. Now deep learning approaches are rapidly gaining popularity and it is just a matter of time before all commercial MT systems are NN based, if they are not already. An early example of the NN approach is that by Kalchbrenner and Blunsom [KB13].

Alignment in seq2seq models was introduced in Dzmitry Bahdanau et al. [BCB14]. This group also seems to be the first to have adopted the now standard term *neural machine translation* for this approach. In this chapter's position-only attention model the model is given only the numeric values for the locations of the French and English words when deciding how much weight to give to the corresponding French state. In [BCB14] the model also has information about the LSTM states at the French and English locations.

As for on-line MT tutorials, one by Thad Luong et al. just came on-line as this book was going to the publisher [TL]. The previous Google seq2seq/MT tutorial was not so great for pedagogical purposes (imagine a cookbook teaching how to make pancakes by saying "mix together 100,000 gallons of milk and a million eggs ..."), but this one looks pretty reasonable and could well make a good foundation for further exploration of neural MT in particular and seq2seq in general.

There are many other tasks besides MT for which seq2seq models have been pressed into service. One that is particularly "hot" right now is *chatbots* — programs that are given conversational expressions and attempt to carry on the conversation. They are also one of the basics of home assistants — e.g., Amazon's Alexa. ("Hot" is definitely the right word here: there is an on-line chatbot magazine and an article entitled "Why Chatbots Are the Future of Marketing.") A possible project on this topic is described in a post by Surlyadeepan Ram [Ram17].

Chapter 6

Deep Reinforcement Learning

Reinforcement learning (abbreviated *RL*) is the branch of machine learning concerned with learning how an *agent* should behave in an *environment* in order to maximize a *reward*. Naturally, *deep* reinforcement learning restricts the learning method to deep learning.

Typically the environment is defined mathematically as a *Markov decision process* (*MDP*). MDPs consist of a set of states $s \in S$ that the agent can be in (e.g., locations on a map), a finite set of actions ($a \in A$), a function $T(s, a, s') = \Pr(S_{t+1} = s' \mid S_t = s, A = a)$ that takes the agent from one state to another, a reward function from a state, action, and subsequent state to the reals $R(s, a, s')$, and a *discount* $\gamma \in [0, 1]$ (to be explained momentarily). In general actions are probabilistic, so T specifies a distribution over the possible resulting state from taking an action in a particular state. The models are called *Markov* decision processes because they make the *Markov assumption* — if we know the current state, the history (how we got to the current state) does not matter.

In MDPs time is discrete. At any time the agent is in some state, takes an action that leads it to a new state, and receives some reward, often zero. The goal is to maximize its *discounted future reward* as defined by

$$\sum_{t=0}^{t=\infty} \gamma^t R(s_t, a_t, s_{t+1}) \tag{6.1}$$

If $\gamma < 1$ then this sum is finite. If γ is missing (or equivalently equal to 1) then the sum can grow to infinity, which complicates the math. A typical γ is .9. The quantity in Equation 6.1 is called *discounted* future reward

113

1. For all s set $V(s) = 0$

2. Repeat until convergence:

   (a) For all s:
       i. For all a, set $Q(s,a) = \sum_{s'} T(s,a,s')(R(s,a,s') + \gamma V(s'))$
       ii. $V(s) = max_a Q(s,a)$

3. return Q

Figure 6.1: The value iteration algorithm

because the repeated multiplication by a quantity less than one causes the model to "discount" (value less highly) rewards in the future compared to rewards we get right now. This is reasonable since nobody lives forever.

Our goal is to *solve* the MDP — we also speak of finding an optimum *policy*. A policy is a function $\pi(s) = a$ that for every state s specifies the action a the agent should take. A policy is optimum, denoted $\pi^*(s)$, if the specified actions lead to the maximum expected discounted future reward. The *expected* here means to find the expected value, as explained in Section 2.4.3. Since actions are not deterministic, the same action may end up giving quite different rewards.

So this chapter is concerned with learning optimal MDP policies: first using so-called *tabular* methods, then using their deep-learning counterparts.

6.1 Value Iteration

A basic question we need to answer before we talk about solving MDPs is whether we assume the agent "knows" the functions T and R or has to wander around the environment learning them as well as creating its policy. It simplifies things greatly if we know T and R, so we start with that case. In this section we also assume there are only a finite number of states s.

Value iteration is about as simple as policy learning in MDPs gets. (In fact, it is arguably not a learning algorithm at all, in that it does not need to get training examples or interact with the environment.) The algorithm is given in Figure 6.1. V is a *value function* a vector of size $|s|$ where each entry $V(s)$ is the best expected discounted reward we can hope for when we start in state s. Q (simply called the *Q function*) is a table of size $|s|$ by $|a|$ in which we store our current estimate of the discounted reward when

0:S	1:F	2:F	3:F
4:F	5:H	6:F	7:H
8:F	9:F	10:F	11:H
12:H	13:F	14:F	15:G

S   starting location

F   frozen location

H   hole

G   goal location

Figure 6.2: The frozen-lake problem

taking action a in state s. The value function V has a real-number value for every state: the higher the number, the better it is to reach that state. Q is more fine-grained: it gives the values we can expect for each state-action pair. If our values in V are correct then line 2(a)i will set $Q(s, a)$ correctly. It says that the value for $Q(s, a)$ consists of the immediate reward $R(s, a.s')$ plus the value for the state we end up in, as specified by V. Since actions are not deterministic, we have to sum over all possible states. This gives us the expectation.

Once we have the correct Q we can determine the optimal policy π by always picking the action $a = \arg\max_{a'} Q(s, a')$. Here $\arg\max_x g(x)$ returns the value of x for which $g(x)$ is maximum.

To make this concrete, we consider a very simple MDP — the *frozen-lake problem*. The game is one of many that are part of the *Open AI Gym* — a group of computer games with uniform APIs convenient for reinforcement learning experimentation. We have a $4 * 4$ grid (the lake) shown in Figure 6.2. The goal of the game is to get from the start position (state 0 at the upper left) to the goal (lower right) without falling through a hole in the ice. We get a reward of 1 whenever we take an action and end up in the goal state. All other state-action-state triples have zero reward. If we end up in a hole state (or the goal state) the game stops and if we play again we go back to the start state. Otherwise we go left (l), down (d), right (r), or up (u) (the numbers zero to three, respectively) with some probability of "slipping" and not going in the intended direction. In fact, the way the Open AI Gym game is programmed an action, e.g., right, takes us with equal probability to any of the immediately adjacent states except the exact opposite (e.g., left), so it is *very* slippery. If an action would make us move off the lake, it instead leaves us in the state from which we started.

0	0	0	0
0	0	0	0
0	0	0	0
0	0	.33	0

0	0	0	0
0	0	0	0
0	0	.1	0
0	.1	.46	0

Figure 6.3: State values after the first and second iterations of value iteration

To compute V and Q for the frozen lake we repeatedly go through all states s and recompute $V(s)$. Consider state 1. This requires computing $Q(1, a)$ for all four actions and then setting $V(1)$ to the maximum of the four Q values. OK, let's start by computing what happens if we choose to move left, $Q(1, l)$. To do this we need to sum over all s' — all the game states. There are 16 states in the game, but starting in state 1 we can only reach three of them with nonzero probability, states 0, 5, and 1 itself (by trying to move up, being blocked by the lake boundary, and thus not moving at all). So, looking only at end states s' that have nonzero $T(1, l, s')$ values, we compute the following sum:

$$Q(1, l) \quad = \quad .33 \cdot (0 + .9 \cdot 0) + ..33 \cdot (0 + .9 \cdot 0) + .33 \cdot (0 + .9 \cdot 0) \quad (6.2)$$
$$= \quad 0 + 0 + 0 \quad (6.3)$$
$$= \quad 0 \quad (6.4)$$

The first of the summands says that when attempting to move left, with probability .33 we end up in state 0. We get zero reward for doing so, and our estimated future reward is $.9 \cdot 0$. This value is zero, as will be the case if instead of going left, we slipped down (and ended up in state 5) or remained in state 1. So $Q(1, l) = 0$. Because the V values for the three states we can reach from state 1 are all 0, $Q(1, d)$, and $Q(1, u)$ are both 0 as well, and line 2(a)ii sets $V(1) = 0$.

In fact, on the first iteration V continues to be zero until we get to state 14, where we finally get nonzero values for $Q(14, d)$, $Q(14, r)$, and $Q(14, u)$:

$$Q(14, d) \quad = \quad .33 \cdot (0 + .9 \cdot 0) + .33 \cdot (0 + .9 \cdot 0) + .33 \cdot (1 + .9 \cdot 0) = .33$$
$$Q(14, r) \quad = \quad .33 \cdot (0 + .9 \cdot 0) + .33 \cdot (0 + .9 \cdot 0) + .33 \cdot (1 + .9 \cdot 0) = .33$$
$$Q(14, u) \quad = \quad .33 \cdot (0 + .9 \cdot 0) + .33 \cdot (0 + .9 \cdot 0) + .33 \cdot (1 + .9 \cdot 0) = .33$$

and $V(14) = .33$.

The left half of Figure 6.3 shows the table of V values after the first iteration. Value iteration is one of several algorithms that work toward an

```
0   import gym
1   game = gym.make('FrozenLake-v0')
2   for i in range(1000):
3       st = game.reset()
4       for stps in range(99):
5           act=np.random.randint(0,4)
6           nst,rwd,dn,_=game.step(act)
7           # update T and R
9           if dn: break
```

Figure 6.4: Collecting statistics for an Open AI Gym game

optimum policy by keeping tables of the best estimates of function values. Hence the name *tabular methods*.

On iteration two, again most values stay 0, but this time states 10 and 13 also get nonzero Q and V entries because from them we can go to state 14 and, as just observed, now $V(14) = .33$. The V values after the second go-round of value iteration are shown on the right-hand side of Figure 6.3.

Another way to think about value iteration is that every change to V (and Q) incorporates exact information about what is going to happen one move into the future (we get reward R) but then falls back to the initially inaccurate information already incorporated into these functions. Eventually the functions include more and more information about states we have not yet reached.

6.2   Q-learning

Value iteration assumes the learner has access to the complete details of the model environment. We now consider the opposite case — *model-free learning*. The agent can explore the environment by making a move, and it gets back information about the reward and the next state, but it does not know the actual movement probabilities or reward function T, R.

Assuming that our environment is a Markov decision process, the most obvious way to plan in a model-free environment is to wander around the environment randomly, collect statistics on T, R, and then create a policy based upon the Q table as described in the last section. Figure 6.4 shows the highlights of a program for doing this. Line 1 creates the frozen-lake

game. To start a game (from the initial state) we call `reset()`. A single
run of the frozen-lake game ends when we either fall in a hole or reach the
goal state. So the outer loop (line 2) specifies that we are going to run the
game 1000 times. The inner loop (line 4) says that for any one game we cut
off the game at 99 steps. (In practice this never happens — we fall into a
hole or reach the goal long before then.) Line 5 says that at each step we
first randomly generate the next action. (There are four possible actions,
left, down, right, and up: the numbers 0 to 3 respectively.) Line 6 is the
critical step. The function `step(act)` takes one argument (the action to be
taken) and returns four values. The first is the state in which the action
has left the game (in FL an integer from 0 to 15) and the second is the
value of the reward we receive (in FL typically 0, occasionally 1). The third
state, named `dn` in the figure, is a true-false indicator whether the run of
the game is terminated (i.e. we fell into a hole or reached the goal). The
last argument is information about the true transition probabilities, which
we ignore if we are doing model-free learning.

If you think about it, wandering at random in the game is a pretty bad
way to collect our statistics. Mostly what happens is that we wander into
a hole and go back to the start and keep collecting statistics about what
happens at the states near the start state. A much better idea is to learn
and wander at the same time, and allow the learning to influence where we
go. If we do, in fact, glean useful information in the process, then as we
progress we get further and further into the game, thus learning more about
more different states. In this section we do this by choosing according to the
probability ϵ either to (a) choose a move at random, or (with probability
$(1 - \epsilon)$) (b) base our decision on the knowledge we have gleaned so far. If ϵ
is fixed this is called an *epsilon-greedy strategy*.

It is also common to have ϵ decrease over time (an *epsilon-decreasing
strategy*). One simple way to do this is to have an associated hyperparameter
E and set $\epsilon = \frac{E}{i+E}$, where i is the number of times we have played the
game. (So E is the number of games in which we go from mostly random to
mostly learned.) As you might expect, how we choose whether to explore
or base our choice on our current understanding of the game can have a
big effect on how fast we learn the game, and has its own name — the
exploration-exploitation tradeoff (when we use game knowledge we are said
to be *exploiting* the knowledge we have already picked up).

Another popular way to combine exploration and exploitation is always
to use the values given by the Q function but turn them into a probability
distribution and then pick an action according to that distribution, rather
than always picking the action with the highest value. (The latter is called

the *greedy algorithm.*) So if we had three actions and their Q values were [4, 1, 1], we would pick the first two-thirds of the time, etc.

Q-learning is one of the first and most popular algorithm for model-free learning combining exploration and exploitation. The basic idea is not to learn R and T but to learn the Q and V tables directly. Now in Figure 6.4 we need to modify lines 5 (we no longer act completely randomly) and line 7, where we we modify Q and V, not R and T.

We have already explained what to do at line 5, so we turn to line 7. Our Q-learning update equations are

$$Q(s, a) = (1 - \alpha)Q(s, a) + \alpha(R(s, a, n) + \gamma V(n)) \qquad (6.5)$$
$$V(s) = \max_{a'} Q(s, a'), \qquad (6.6)$$

where s is the state we were occupying, a is the action we took, and a' is the state we now occupy, having just taken a step in the game in line 6 of Figure 6.4.

The new value of $Q(s, a)$ is a mixture controlled by α of its old value and the new information — so α is sort of a learning rate. Typically α is small. To make it clear why it is needed, it is useful to contrast these equations with lines 2(a)i and 2(a)ii from the value iteration algorithm in Figure 6.1. There, since the algorithm was given R and T, we could sum over all possible outcomes of the action we took. In Q-learning we cannot to this. All we have is the last outcome of taking a step. The new information is based upon just one move in our exploration of the environment. Suppose we are state 14 of Figure 6.2 but unbeknownst to us there is a very small probability (.0001) that if we move down from that state we get a "reward" of –10. The odds are this is not going to happen, but if it does it will throw things very badly out of whack. The moral is that the algorithm should not put too much emphasis on a single move. In value iteration we know both T and R, and between the two of them the algorithm factors in both the possibility of a negative reward and the low probability of its happening.

6.3 Basic Deep-Q Learning

With tabular Q learning under our belt we are now in position to understand *deep-Q learning.* As in the tabular version, we start with the schema of Figure 6.4. The big change this time is that we represent the Q function not as a table but using a NN model.

In Chapter 1 we briefly mentioned that machine learning can be characterized as a *function-approximation problem*— finding a function that closely matches some target functions; e.g., the target function might map from pixels to one of ten integers, where the pixels are from an image of the corresponding digit. We are given the value of the function for some inputs and the goal is to create a function that closely matches its output for all those values, and by doing so to fill in the values of the function at places where we were not given its value. In the case of deep-Q learning the function-approximation analogy is completely apt — we are going to approximate our (unknown) Q function using NNs by wandering around the Markov decision process, learning along the way.

We should emphasize that the change from tabular to deep-learning models is *not* motivated by the frozen-lake example, which is exactly the sort of problem for which tabular Q learning is suited. Deep-Q learning is needed when there are too many states to create a table for them.

One of the events in the reemergence of NNs was the creation of a single NN model that could apply deep-Q learning to many Atari games. This program was created by *DeepMind*, a startup in 2014 purchased by Google. DeepMind was able to get a single program to learn a bunch of different games by representing the games in terms of the pixels in the images that the games generate. Each pixel combination is a state. Offhand I do not remember the image size they used, but even if it were as small as the $28 * 28$ images we used for Mnist, and each pixel was either on or off, that would be 2^{784} possible pixel value combinations — so in principle that number of states would be needed in the Q table. At any rate, it's way too many for a tabular scheme to cover. (I looked it up: an Atari game window is $210 * 160$ RGB, and the DeepMind program reduced this to $84 * 84$ black and white.) We return later to discuss cases more complicated than frozen-lake.

Replacing the Q table by a NN function boils down to this: to get a movement recommendation, rather than look in the Q table, we in effect call the Q table by feeding the state into a one-layer NN, as shown in Figure 6.5. The TF code for creating just the Q-function model parameters is given in Figure 6.6. We feed in the current state (the scalar `inptSt`), which we turn into the one-hot vector `oneH` that is transformed by a single layer of linear units `Q`. `Q` has the shape $16 * 4$ where 16 is the size of the one-hot vector of states and 4 is the number of possible actions. The output `qVals` are the entries in $Q(s)$, and `outAct`, the maximum of the Q table entries, is the policy recommendation.

Implicit in Figure 6.6 is the assumption we are playing only one game at a time, and thus when we feed in an input state (and get out a policy recommendation) there is only one of them. From our normal handling of NNs, this corresponds to a batch size of one. For example, the input state,

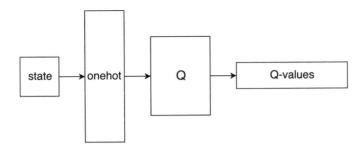

Figure 6.5: Frozen-lake deep-Q-learning NN

```
inptSt = tf.placeholder(dtype=tf.int32)
oneH=tf.one_hot(inptSt,16)
Q= tf.Variable(tf.random_uniform([16,4],0,0.01))
qVals= tf.matmul([oneH],Q)
outAct= tf.argmax(qVals,1)
```

Figure 6.6: TF model parameters for the Q learning function

inptSt, is a scalar — the number of the state in which the actor finds itself. From this it follows that oneH is a vector. Then, since matmul expects two matrices, we call it with [oneH]. This in turn means that qVals is going to be a matrix of shape $[1, 4]$, i.e., it will only have the Q values for one action (up, down, etc.). Last, then, outAct is of shape $[1]$, so the action recommendation is outAct[0]. (You should see why we go into this much detail when we present the rest of the code for deep-Q learning in Figure 6.7.)

As in tabular Q learning, the algorithm chooses an action either at random (at the beginning of the learning process) or on the basis of the Q-table recommendation (near the end). In deep-Q learning we get the Q-table recommendation by feeding the current state s into the NN of Figure 6.5 and choosing an action u, d, r, or l, according to which of the four is the highest. Once we have the action, we call step to get the result and then learn from it. Naturally, to do this in deep learning we need a loss function.

But now that we mention it, *what is the loss function of deep-Q learning?* This is the key question because, as has been evident all along, as we make moves, particularly in the early learning stages, we do not know whether they are good or bad! However, we do know the following: on average

$$R(s, a) + \gamma \max_{a'} Q(s', a') \tag{6.7}$$

(where as before, s' is the state we end up in after a in s) is a more accurate estimate of $Q(s, a)$ than the current value, because we are looking one move ahead. So we make the loss

$$(Q(s, a) - (R(s, a) + \gamma \max_{a'} Q(s', a')))^2, \tag{6.8}$$

the square of the difference between what just happened (when we took the step) and predicted values (from the Q table/function). This is called the *squared-error loss* or *quadratic loss*. The difference between the Q calculated by the network (the first term) and the value we can compute by observing the actual reward for the next action plus the Q value one step in the future (the second term) is called the *temporal difference error*, or *TD(0)*. If we looked two steps into the future it would be TD(1).

Figure 6.7 gives the rest of the TF code (following on from that in Figure 6.6). The first five lines build the remainder of the TF graph. Now skim the rest of the code with emphasis on lines 7, 11, 13, 14, 19, and 25. They implement the basic AI Gym "wandering." That is, they correspond to all of Figure 6.4. We create the game (line 7) and play 2000 individual games (line 11), each one starting with `game.reset()` (line 13). Each episode has a maximum of 99 moves (line 14). The actual move is made in line 19. The game is over as indicated by the flag we named `dn` (line 25).

This leaves two gaps, lines 15–17 (choose next action) and 20–22. Line 15 is the forward pass in which we give the NN the current state and get back a vector of length 1 (which the next line turns into a scalar — the number of the action). We also always give the program a small probability of taking a random action (line 18). This ensures that eventually we explore all the game space. Lines 20–22 are concerned with computing the loss and performing the backward pass to update the model parameters. This is also the point of lines 1–5, which create the TF graph for loss computation and updating.

The performance of this program is not as good as that of tabular Q learning but, as we said, tabular methods are quite suitable for the frozen-lake MDP.

```
1  nextQ = tf.placeholder(shape=[1,4],dtype=tf.float32)
2  loss = tf.reduce_sum(tf.square(nextQ - qVals))
3  trainer = tf.train.GradientDescentOptimizer(learning_rate=0.1)
4  updateMod = trainer.minimize(loss)
5  init = tf.global_variables_initializer()

6  gamma = .99
7  game=gym.make('FrozenLake-v0')
8  rTot=0
9  with tf.Session() as sess:
10  sess.run(init)
11  for i in range(2000):
12    e = 50.0/(i + 50)
13    s=game.reset()
14    for j in range(99):
15     nActs,nxtQ=sess.run([outAct,qVals],feed_dict={inptSt: s})
16     nAct=nActs[0]
17     if np.random.rand(1)<e: nAct= game.action_space.sample()
19     s1,rwd,dn,_ = game.step(nAct)
20     Q1 = sess.run(qVals,feed_dict={inptSt: s1})
21     nxtQ[0,nAct] = rwd + gamma*(np.max(Q1))
22     sess.run(updateMod,feed_dict={inptSt:s, nextQ:nxtQ})
23     rTot+=rwd
24     if dn: break
25     s = s1
26 print "Percent games succesful: ", rTot/2000
```

Figure 6.7: Remainder of deep-Q-learning code

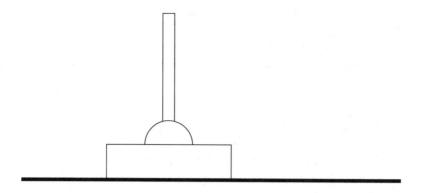

Figure 6.8: A cart pole

6.4 Policy Gradient Methods

We now turn to an Open AI Gym problem that cannot be handled by standard tabular methods, *cart pole*, and a new-deep RL method, *policy gradients*. A "cart pole," as shown in Figure 6.8, is a cart on a one-dimensional track. It has a pole attached to it by a sticky joint so that when the cart is propelled in one direction or another the top of the pole moves left or right according to the dictates of Newton's laws. A state consists of four values — the postion of the cart and the angle of the pole after the previous and current move. We give values at consecutive times to enable the program to figure out the direction of motion. There are two actions the player can make: propel the cart to the right or to the left. The impulse always has the same magnitude. Should the cart move too far to the right or left, or should the top of the pole move too far from perpendicular, `step` signals that the current game is over, and we need to `reset` to start a new one. We get one unit of reward for every move we make before failing. Naturally, the goal is to keep the cart and pole well positioned for as long as possible. Since the state corresponds to a four-tuple of real numbers, the number of possible states is infinite, so tabular methods are ruled out.

So far we have used our NN models to approximate the Q function for our MDP. In this section we show a method in which the NN models the policy function directly. Again we are concerned with model-free learning, and again we adopt the paradigm of wandering around the game environment, initially choosing actions mostly at random but moving over to using the NN recommendation. As pretty much everywhere in this chapter, the burning problem is finding an appropriate loss function, since we do not know the correct actions we ought to be taking.

In deep-Q learning we make one move at a time, and we depend on the fact that, having made the move, received a reward, and ended up in a new state, our knowledge of the current local environment has improved. Our loss was the difference between what was predicted (e.g., the Q function) on the basis of the old knowledge and what, in fact, happened.

Here we try something different. Suppose we play an entire iteration of a game without making any modification to our network — e.g., we make 20 moves (directions to the cart) before the pole tips over. This time we handle exploration/exploitation by choosing actions according to a probability distribution derived from the Q function, rather than taking the Q function maximum.

Under this scenario we can compute the discounted reward for the first state $(D_0(\mathbf{s}, \mathbf{a}))$ when it is followed by all the states and actions we just tried out:

$$D_0(\mathbf{s}, \mathbf{a}) = \sum_{t=0}^{n-1} \gamma^t R(s_t, a_t, s_{t+1}) \tag{6.9}$$

If we took n steps we can compute the future discounted reward for any of the state-action combinations s_i, a_i from the recurrence relation

$$D_n(\mathbf{s}, \mathbf{a}) = 0 \tag{6.10}$$
$$D_i(\mathbf{s}, \mathbf{a}) = R(s_i, a_i, s_{i+1}) + \gamma D_{i+1}(\mathbf{s}, \mathbf{a}) \tag{6.11}$$

That is, the discounted future reward for, e.g., the fourth state in the sequence of states we move through (when taking action a) is D_4. Again, note we have gained information here. For example, before we tried the first random sequence of moves we had no idea what a possible reward was. Afterward we know that, say, 10 is possible (and indeed reasonable for a random action sequence). Or then again, we now know if we fell over on move 10, then $Q(s_9, a_9) = 0$.

A good loss function that captures these facts and many others is:

$$L(\mathbf{s}, \mathbf{a}) = \sum_{t=0}^{n-1} D_t(\mathbf{s}, \mathbf{a})(-\log \Pr(a_t \mid s))) \tag{6.12}$$

To unpack this, first note that the rightmost term is the cross-entropy loss, and by itself has the effect of encouraging the net to respond with action a_t when it is in state s_t. Of course, by itself this is pretty useless since, particularly at the beginning of learning, we chose the actions randomly.

Next consider how the D_t values affect this. In particular, suppose a_0 was a bad reaction to s_0. For example, suppose the cart is centered, and

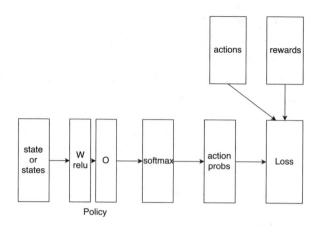

Figure 6.9: Deep learning architecture for REINFORCE

the pole is learning to the right at the start, and we chose to go left, making the pole lean still further to the right. The reader should see that, all else equal, the value of D_0 is smaller in this case than it would have been if we had chosen to move right — the reason being that (all else equal) if the first move is good, the pole and cart should remain in bounds longer (n is larger) and the D values are larger. So Equation 6.12 gives a higher loss to a bad a_0 than a good one, thus training the NN to prefer the good one.

This architecture/loss-function combination is known as *REINFORCE*. Figure 6.9 shows the basic architecture. The important thing to notice is that the NN here is used in two different ways. First, looking at the left-hand side, we give the NN a single state which, as mentioned earlier, is a four-tuple of reals indicating the position and velocity of the cart and the pole-head. In this mode we get out probabilities for taking the two possible actions, as indicated in the middle-right of the figure. When in this mode we do not provide the placeholder for the rewards or actions with values since (a) we don't know them, and (b) we don't need them since we are not computing the loss at this point. After we have made all the moves for an entire game, we use the NN in the other mode. This time we give it the sequence of actions and the rewards, and this time we ask it to compute the loss and perform back propagation. In training mode we are, in a sense, computing actions in two different ways. First, we give the NN the states we go through, and for each state, the policy computation layers compute the action probabilities. Second, we directly feed in the actions taken as a placeholder. This is because when deciding on actions in game-playing

```
state= tf.placeholder(shape=[None,4],dtype=tf.float32)
W =tf.Variable(tf.random_uniform([4,8],dtype=tf.float32))
hidden= tf.nn.relu(tf.matmul(state,W))
O= tf.Variable(tf.random_uniform([8,2],dtype=tf.float32))
output= tf.nn.softmax(tf.matmul(hidden,O))

rewards = tf.placeholder(shape=[None],dtype=tf.float32)
actions = tf.placeholder(shape=[None],dtype=tf.int32)
indices = tf.range(0, tf.shape(output)[0]) * 2 + actions
actProbs = tf.gather(tf.reshape(output, [-1]), indices)
aloss = -tf.reduce_mean(tf.log(actProbs)*rewards)
trainOp= tf.train.AdamOptimizer(.01).minimize(aloss)
```

Figure 6.10: TF graph instructions for cart-pole policy gradient NN

mode we do not necessarily pick the action with the highest probability, but rather choose randomly based upon the action probabilities. To compute the loss according to Equation 6.12 we need both.

Figure 6.10 gives TF code for creating the policy gradient NN using the loss function in Equation 6.12, and Figure 6.11 gives pseudocode for using the NN to learn a policy and act in the game environment. First consider the pseudocode. Note that the outermost loop (line 2) has us playing 3001 sessions of the game. The inner loop (line 2b) has us playing the game session until **step** tells us we are done (line D) or until we have moved 999 times. We choose a random action according to probabilities derived from our NN (lines i, ii) and then execute the action in the game. We save the results in the list **hist** so we have a record of what happened. If the action leads to a final state we then update the model parameters.

We see from Figure 6.10 that **output** is computed by taking the current-state values **state** and running them through a two-layer NN with linear units W and O naturally separated by a **tf.relu**, and then fed into a **softmax** to turn the logits into probabilities. As should be familiar from previous uses of multilayer NNs, the first layer has dimensions [input-size, hidden-size], and the second [hidden-size, output-size] where hidden-size is a hyperparameter (we chose 8).

Because we have designed a new loss function here and not used a standard one from the TF library, the loss computation had to be built up from more basic TF functions (second half of Figure 6.10). For example, in all our previous NNs the forward and backward pass were inextricably linked

1. totRs=[ ]

2. for i in range(3001):

    (a) st=reset game

    (b) for j in range(999):

        i. actDist = sess.run(output, feed_dict=state:[st])

        ii. select act randomly according to actDist

        iii. st1,r,dn,_=game.step(act)

        iv. collect st,a,r in hist

        v. st=st1

        vi. if dn:

            A. disRs = [D_i(states, actions from hst) | i = 0 to j - 1]

            B. create feed_dict with state=st, actions, from hist and rewards=disRs.

            C. sess.run(trainOp,feed_dict=feed_dict)

            D. add j to end of totRs

            E. break

        vii. if i%100=0: print out average of last 100 entries in totRs

Figure 6.11: Pseudocode for a policy-gradient-training NN for cart pole

$$
\begin{array}{cc}
\Pr(\texttt{l} \mid s_1) & \Pr(\texttt{r} \mid s_1) \\
\Pr(\texttt{l} \mid s_2) & \Pr(\texttt{r} \mid s_2) \\
& \\
\Pr(\texttt{l} \mid s_n) & \Pr(\texttt{r} \mid s_n)
\end{array}
\quad \rightarrow \quad
\begin{array}{c}
Pr(a_1 \mid s_1) \\
Pr(a_2 \mid s_2) \\
\\
Pr(a_n \mid s_n)
\end{array}
$$

Figure 6.12: Extracting action probabilities from the tensor of all probabilities

insofar as no computations from outside TF were involved. Here we are getting the values of **reward** from the outside — **reward** is a placeholder, fed in according to lines A, B, and C in Figure 6.11. Similarly, **actions** is a placeholder.

In the last three lines of Figure 6.10 things look more familiar. **loss** is just computing the quantities from Equation 6.12. For **optimizer** we have used the *Adam optimizer*. We could have used our familiar gradient-descent optimizer by just substituting it in and doubling the learning rate, and we would have achieved almost as good performance, but not quite. The Adam optimizer is slightly more complicated and generally considered superior. It differs from gradient descent in several ways, the most fundamental being the use of *momentum*. As the name suggests, an optimizer that uses momentum tends to keep moving a parameter value up/down if it has been moving up/down recently — more so than gradient descent would do.

This leaves the middle two lines of Figure 6.10, the ones setting **indices** and **actProbs**. First, ignore how they work, and concentrate on what they need to do. What is needed is the transformation shown in Figure 6.12. On the left we see the output of a forward pass computing the probability that each of the possible actions **r** and **l** is the best one to take. If this were Chapter 1 and we had full supervision, we would multiply this by a batch-size tensor of one-hot vectors to get the probabilities of the actions we should take according to the supervision. This is, in fact, what we show on the right of Figure 6.12.

To enact this transformation we depend on **gather**, which takes two arguments,

```
tf.gather(tensor, indices)
```

and pulls out the elements of the tensor specified by the numeric indices and puts them together in a new tensor. For example, if **tensor** is $((1,3), (4,6), (2,1), (3,3))$, and **indices** is $(3,1,3)$, then the output is $((3,3), (4,6), (3,3))$. In our case we turn the action probability matrix on the left of Figure

6.12 into a vector of probabilities, and depend on the previous line to set `indicies` to the correct list, so `tf.gather` collects the probabilities of just the actions specified by the vector `actions`. Showing that `indices` is set correctly is left as an exercise for the reader (Exercise 6.5).

It is useful to go back and look more carefully at how Q-learning and REINFORCE are related. First, they differ in how they collect environment information to inform the NN. Q-learning moves one step, and then looks to see if the NN prediction of the outcome is close to what actually occurred. Looking back at Equation 6.8, the Q-learning loss function, we see that if the prediction and outcome are the same, then there is nothing to update. With REINFORCE, on the other hand, we play an entire episode before changing any NN parameters, where an *episode* is a complete run of game, from the initial state until the game signals that it is done. Notice that we could have done something like Q learning but used the REINFORCE parameter modification schedule. This slows down the learning insofar as we make parameter changes much less often, but in compensation we make better changes because we are computing the *actual* discounted reward.

6.5   Actor-Critic Methods

Having just looked at the differences between Q learning and REINFORCE, we now concentrate on the similarities. In both the NN is computing either a policy or, in Q-learning, a function that can be trivially used to create a policy (for any state s always take the action a that maximizes $Q(s, a)$). Thus in both cases our NN is approximating a single function, one that tells us how to act. We call such RL programs *actor* methods. In this section we consider programs that have two NN subcomponents, each with its own loss functions: one as before is an actor program, and the second a *critic* program. As you might guess, we call this type of RL *actor-critic methods*. In particular, in this section we cover the *advantage actor-critic* method, or *a2c*. It is a good choice for us because (a) it works quite well and (b) we can approach it incrementally starting from from REINFORCE. We call the first version (increment) *a2c−*. We again apply it to the cart-pole game.

The method is called *advantage* actor-critic because it uses the notion of "advantage." The advantage of a state-action pair is the difference between the state-action Q value and the state's value:

$$A(s, a) = Q(s, a) - V(s) \qquad (6.13)$$

Intuitively we expect the advantage to be a negative number because in, say, value iteration, $V(s)$ is computed by doing an $\arg\max_a$ over the possible actions. However, for good actions, A is large as negative numbers go, so A measures how good an action is in a particular state compared to the state overall.

Next we define the loss a2c incurs from exploring a sequence of actions from a start state to the end of a game as follows:

$$L_A(\mathbf{s}, \mathbf{a}) = \sum_{t=0}^{n-1} A(s_t, a_t)(-\log \Pr(a_t \mid s_t)))$$ (6.14)

This is very close to the REINFORCE loss of Equation 6.12 but we have replaced $D_t(s, a)$, the discounted reward, by $A_t(s, a)$. We have called this loss L_A to differentiate it from the total loss for a2c, which, as we see below, encompasses a second loss L_C having to do with the critic.

We remember that REINFORCE's loss is meant to encourage actions that lead to larger reward. Now we are encouraging actions that are better than alternative actions from the same state. While this is somewhat reasonable, why should it be better than encouraging high-reward actions directly?

The answer has to do with the variance of $A(s, a)$. As noted in Section 2.4.3, the variance of a function is the expectation of the square of the difference between the function's value and its mean value. Intuitively, this means that functions that vary a lot have high variance, and compared to Q, A should have much lower variance. Look at cart pole. Assuming the game gives us reasonable response in terms of moving left or right compared to how fast the pole moves, the difference between a move right and a move left will be small, and thus A is small in virtually all parts of the state space. Contrast this with Q. A cart-pole game after learning from 100 games is averaging about 20 moves before failing, whereas an even moderately good policy gives us 200 or more.

Add now a second fact — all else equal, it is easier to approximate a function with low variance than one with high. A constant function with zero variance is the easiest of all. So if A is much easier to estimate, that could overcome the disadvantage incurred by maximizing A rather than Q directly. This seems to be the case. Of course, we don't know how to compute A at this point. So that is next on our agenda.

As you remember, in REINFORCE we follow a path based upon our current policy to the end of a game, and use the discounted reward $D_t(s.a)$ from Equation 6.11 to estimate $Q(s, a)$. We now put this to double duty as our estimate of Q when computing A (Equation 6.13). As for $V(s)$, we

```
V1 =tf.Variable(tf.random_normal([4,8],dtype=tf.float32,stddev=.1))
v1Out= tf.nn.relu(tf.matmul(state,V1))
V2 =tf.Variable(tf.random_normal([8,1],dtype=tf.float32,stddev=.1))
v2Out= tf.matmul(v1Out,V2)
advantage = rewards-v2Out
aLoss = -tr.reduce_mean(tf.log(actProbs) * advantage)
cLoss=tf.reduce_mean(tf.square(rewards-vOut))
loss=aLoss + cLoss
```

Figure 6.13: TF code added to Figures 6.10 and 6.11 for a2c

build into our NN a subnetwork just to compute it.

Figure 6.13 gives the extra TF network building code beyond that required for REINFORCE (Figure 6.10). We have created a two-layer fully connected NN, `v1Out` and `v2Out` to compute V, the value function — the critic. It is trained to produce good estimates of V by using a quadratic loss on the disparity between the actual rewards found and the output of the NN approximation (`cLoss`). The actor loss here is from Equation 6.14 and so uses the advantage function. These relatively small changes turn our REINFORCE into a2c–.

Moving beyond a2c–, actual a2c incorporates two further improvements. One problem with REINFORCE (inherited by a2c–) is that it needs to play an entire game before any learning takes place. At the beginning of cart-pole, with a game only lasting 10–20 moves, this is not much of a limitation. But REINFORCE games end up one or two hundred moves long, and a2c– games are longer still. A2c can improve on this by updating the model's parameters much earlier, and more often.

The trick is to pause game execution every, say, 50 (a hyperparameter) actions to update the model parameters. We could not do this in REIN-FORCE. After all, the point of following an entire game's worth of actions was to get a good estimate of Q values for the actions we performed. But a2c allows us to make an estimate by simply adding together (a) the actual rewards we accumulated over the last 50 moves and (b) the V value of the state we end up in. We then zero out `hist` and restart it from scratch with the 51st move, only to repeat it again 50 moves later. (Taken to an extreme, this can also relieve a2c of REINFORCE's requirement that it be used only on games with explicit game restarts.)

A second improvement in full a2c is the use of multiple environments. We noted early on that running a batch of training examples is advantageous insofar as it allows better use of fast matrix-multiplication abilities. Playing a single game at a time does not permit this when computing the next game action. Playing multiple games is equivalent of batching examples in this regard.

6.6 Experience Replay

We mentioned early on that a major catalyst in the rebirth of NNs was DeepMind's success with a program that could play multiple Atari games at an expert level. The NN technology used there is known as *DQN* (*Deep Q Network*). This particular RL scheme has been largely replaced by actor-critic methods, but the program also introduced several improvements that are orthogonal to use of actor vs. actor-critic methods. One in particular is *experience replay*.

As you might expect, RL is a big component of the current push toward self-driving cars. One big problem in the application of RL to this domain is the acquisition of training data. Current RL requires a lot of it, and compared to computers the real world, and in particular streets and highways, move very slowly. Actually, if you start timing Open AI Gym games, even computer simulations can be slow — a large fraction of the time spent in RL is in the execution of the game. If we could speed up the world we could learn even faster, but we can't.

In experience replay we use the same training data multiple times. This is simplest to explain in the context of Open AI Gym. Going back to RE-INFORCE, as we played the game we used a variable `hist` to record the history of a play of the game — each state we occupied, the action we took, the state we ended up in, and the reward received. We needed this at the end of the game play to compute the D_ts, but having computed them we threw the history away. With experience replay, for each time t we save $< s_t, a_t, s_{t+1}, D_t >$. With these numbers we can do another forward and backward pass on our data and get more "juice" out of it. And there is a second benefit as well: we can play, and then replay, each time step in a random order. You may remember the iid assumption mentioned in Section 1.6 where we noted how RL could be particularly problematic as the training examples were correlated from the get-go. Taking random actions from several different game plays reduces this problem significantly.

Of course, we pay a price. An old training example is not as informative as a new one. Furthermore, the data can sort of go stale. Suppose we have data from early in our training before we knew not to, say, move left when the pole is leaning far to the right. And suppose since then we have learned better. This means that we are uselessly relearning from the old data what to do in state s_{old} when, in fact, our current policy never allows us to arrive at that state. So instead we do something like this: keep a buffer of 50 game plays corresponding to, say, 5000 state-action-state-reward four-tuples (we are averaging 100 moves before failing). We now pick, e.g., 400 states at random to train from. We then replace the oldest game in the buffer with a new game played using the new policy based upon the up-to-date parameters.

6.7   References and Further Readings

Reinforcement learning had a rich body of theory and practice long before the advent of deep learning, and deep learning has not supplanted it. After all, the major problem in RL is how to learn when you have only indirect information about which moves are good vs. bad, and deep learning only moves that issue to the question how to define the loss function. It does not say much, if anything, about the nature of the solution. The classic text on RL is that by Richard Sutton and Andrew Barto [SB98]. I myself largely made do with an early tutorial paper by Kaelbling et al. [KLM96] for the pre-deep-learning material herein.

For post-deep learning, early in my reinforcement-learning education I came across Arthur Juliani's blog on the topic. If you go to his blog, particularly parts 0 [Jul16a] and 2 [Jul16b], you will observe that my presentations of cart-pole and REINFORCE are significantly influenced by his, and his code was a starting point for mine. Which reminds me, the original paper on REINFORCE is by Ronald Williams [Wil92].

The a2c reinforcement learning algorithm was proposed as a variant of the *Asynchronous Advantage Actor-Critic (a3c)* algorithm. We noted on page 132 that a2c allows multiple environments to make better use of matrix multiplication software and hardware. In a3c these environments are evaluated asynchronously, presumably to better mix up the state-action combinations that the learner may observe [MBM+16]. This same paper also proposed the a2c algorithm as a subcomponent of a3c. Eventually it was shown to work just as well, and it is much simpler.

6.8   Written Exercises

Exercise 6.1: Show that the V table shown on the right-hand side of Figure 6.3 gives the correct values (to two significant digits) for the state values after the second pass of value iteration.

Exercise 6.2: Equation 6.5 has a parameter α, but our TF implementation in Figures 6.6 and 6.7 seemingly makes no mention of α. Explain where it it "hiding" and what value we gave it.

Exercise 6.3: Suppose that in the training phase of the cart-pole REIN-FORCE algorithm it only took three actions (l,l,r) to reach termination, and $\Pr(l \mid s_1) = .2$, $\Pr(l \mid s_2) = .3$, $\Pr(r \mid s_3) = .9$. Show the values of output, actions, indices, and actProbs.

Exercise 6.4: In REINFORCE we first select actions that take us from the beginning of a cart-pole game until (typically) the pole tips over or the cart goes out of bounds. We do this without updating parameters. We save those actions and, in effect, go through the entire scenario all over again, this time computing loss and updating parameters. Note that if we had saved the actions *and their softmax probabilities* then we could compute the loss without doing all the computation that feeds into the loss function a second time. Explain why this nevertheless does not work — why REINFORCE would not learn anything if we did this without the duplicated computation.

Exercise 6.5: The TF function tf.range when given two arguments

    tf.range(start, limit)

creates a vector of integers starting at start and going up to (but not including) limit. Unless the named variable delta is set, the integers differ by one. Thus its use in Figure 6.10 produces a list of integers in the range 0 to batch-size. Explain how they combined with the next line of TF to accomplish the transformation in Figure 6.12.

Chapter 7

Unsupervised Neural-Network Models

This book has followed a mostly unacknowledged path from *supervised learning* problems such as Mnist to weakly supervised learning problems, such as seq2seq learning and reinforcement learning. Our digit-recognition problem is said to be fully supervised because each training example comes along with the correct answer. In our reinforcement learning examples the training examples are unlabeled. Instead, we get a weak form of labeling insofar as the rewards we get from Open AI Gym guide the learning process. In this chapter we consider *unsupervised learning*, where we get no labels or other forms of supervision. We want to learn the structure of our data from only the data itself. In particular, we look at *autoencoders* (abbreviated *AE*s) and *generative adversarial networks* (or *GAN*s).

7.1   Basic Autoencoding

An autoencoder is a function whose output is, if working correctly, almost identical to the input. For us this function is a neural net. To make this nontrivial, we place obstacles in its way, the most common method being *dimensionality reduction*. Figure 7.1 shows a simple two-layer AE. The input (say a 28*28-pixel Mnist image) is passed though a layer of linear units and is transformed into the intermediate vector, which is significantly smaller than the original input — e.g., 256 compared to the original 784. This vector is then itself put through a second layer, and the goal is for the output of the second layer to be identical to the input of the first. The reasoning goes that to the degree we can reduce the dimensions of the middle layer compared

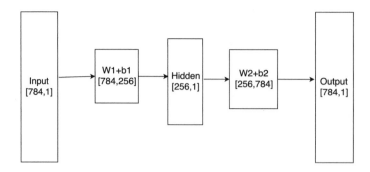

Figure 7.1: A simple two-layer AE

to the input, the NN has encoded information in the middle layer about the structure of Mnist images. To put this at a greater level of abstraction, we have:

$$\text{input} \rightarrow \text{encoder} \rightarrow \text{hidden} \rightarrow \text{decoder} \rightarrow \text{input}$$

where the *encoder* looks like a task-oriented NN and the *decoder* looks like the encoder in reverse. The encoding process is also called *downsampling* (as it reduces image size) and the decoder process *upsampling*.

We care about AEs for several reasons. One is simply theoretical, and perhaps psychological. Except in school, people get little by way of supervision for learning, and by the time we enter school we have already learned the most important of our skills: vision, spoken language, motor tasks, and at its most basic, planning. Presumably this is possible only through *un*supervised learning.

A more practical reason is the use of *pre-training* or *co-training*. Labeled training data is usually in short supply, and our models almost always work better the more parameters they have to manipulate. Pre-training is the technique of training some of the parameters first on a related task, then starting the main training cycles not with our now standard random initialization, but rather from values reached when trained on the related task. Co-training works much the same way, except we do the training and "pretraining" at the same time. That is, the NN model has two loss functions that are summed to get the total loss. One is the "real" loss that minimizes the number of errors in the problem we really want to solve. The other is for a related problem, which could just be reproducing some or all the data we are using — an autoencoding problem.

A third reason for studying autoencoding is a variant called *variational*

	7	8	9	10	11	12	13	14	15	16	17	18	19	20
0	0	0	0	0	0	0	0	0	0	0	0	0	0	0
1	0	0	0	0	0	0	0	0	0	0	0	0	0	0
2	0	0	0	0	0	0	0	0	0	0	0	0	0	0
3	0	0	0	0	0	0	0	0	0	0	0	0	0	0
4	0	0	0	0	0	0	0	0	0	0	0	0	0	0
5	0	0	0	0	0	0	0	0	0	0	0	0	0	0
6	3	14	15	1	0	0	0	0	0	0	0	0	0	0
7	187	221	205	151	74	11	1	0	0	2	8	23	55	69
8	237	249	251	250	249	239	221	225	197	214	216	236	237	228
9	92	194	232	219	225	245	251	251	249	251	241	237	249	250
10	1	8	7	17	31	49	100	126	106	45	37	81	242	251
11	0	0	0	0	1	9	13	7	2	0	1	43	239	247
12	0	0	0	0	0	2	2	0	0	0	2	151	247	215
13	0	0	0	0	0	0	0	0	0	1	61	246	248	57
14	0	0	0	0	0	0	0	0	1	32	207	253	185	10
15	0	0	0	0	0	0	0	0	9	176	251	237	31	1
16	0	0	0	0	0	0	0	0	47	237	252	67	2	0
17	0	0	0	0	1	0	1	9	171	249	237	9	0	0
18	0	0	2	7	1	1	5	100	243	251	138	1	0	0
19	0	0	0	2	1	0	19	217	253	222	19	0	0	0
20	0	0	0	0	0	2	107	246	241	44	1	0	0	0
21	0	0	0	0	1	48	220	247	168	4	0	0	0	0
22	0	0	0	0	18	196	251	233	42	0	0	0	0	0
23	0	0	0	1	98	249	250	140	2	0	0	0	0	0
24	0	0	0	14	237	254	242	40	0	0	0	0	0	0
25	0	0	5	116	252	254	205	8	0	0	0	0	0	0
26	0	0	16	158	253	249	56	4	2	0	1	0	0	0
27	0	0	0	0	2	1	0	0	0	0	0	0	0	0

Figure 7.2: Reconstruction of Mnist test example in Figure 1.1

autoencoders. They are like standard ones, except they are designed to return random images in the style of those on which the AE was trained. A video-game designer may have the action of the game take place in a city, but would rather not spend the time separately designing, say, a few hundred buildings in which to set the action. Good variational autoencoders these days can be entrusted with this task. In the long run we may hope for much better ones that might produce new novels that read like Hemingway or your favorite detective series.

We start with basic autoencoding where we are simply reconstructing the input — Minist digits. Figure 7.2 shows the output of a four-layer AE when the input is the image of a 7 at the very start of Chapter 1. The autoencoder can be expressed as:

$$\mathbf{h} = S(S(\mathbf{x}\mathbf{E}_1 + \mathbf{e}_1)\mathbf{E}_2 + \mathbf{e}_2) \tag{7.1}$$

$$\mathbf{o} = S(\mathbf{h}\mathbf{D}_1 + \mathbf{d}_1)\mathbf{D}_2 + \mathbf{d}_2 \tag{7.2}$$

$$L = \sum_{i=1}^{n}(x_i - o_i)^2 \tag{7.3}$$

We have two fully connected encoding layers, the first with weights $\mathbf{E}_1, \mathbf{e}_1$, the second with $\mathbf{E}_2, \mathbf{e}_2$. In the creation of the reconstructed 7 in Figure 7.2 the first layer has shape [784, 256] and the second [256,128], so the final image size has 128 "pixels," i.e., it is sort of like an image of height and width equal to $\sqrt{128}$. Equation 7.3 states that we are using squared-error loss, which makes sense in that we are trying to predict pixel values, not class membership. We use S, the sigmoid function, for our nonlinearity.

You might wonder why we used a sigmoid activation function rather than our almost standard `relu`. The reason is that so far we have not been much concerned with the actual values that get passed through the network: at the end they are all passed through the softmax function and mostly all that remains are their relative values. An AE, in contrast, compares the absolute values of the input against those of the output. As you may remember when we discussed the data normalization of our Mnist images (19), we divided the raw pixel values by 255 to normalize their values from 0 to 1. As we saw in Figure 2.7, the sigmoid function ranges from 0 at the low end to 1 at the top. Since this exactly matches the range of pixel values, it means that the NN does not have to learn to put values in this range — rather the range is "built in." Naturally this makes learning to produce these values easier than with `relu`, which has the lower constraint but not the upper.

Since autoencoders have multiple fairly similar layers (in this case they are all fully connected), the `layers` module discussed in Section 2.4.4 is particularly useful here. In particular, note that the model outlined in Equations 7.1–7.3 can be succinctly coded as:

```
E1=layers.fully_connected(img,256,tf.sigmoid)
E2=layers.fully_connected(E1,128,tf.sigmoid)
D2=layers.fully_connected(E2,256,tf.sigmoid)
D1=layers.fully_connected(D2,784,tf.softmax)
```

where we assume that our image, `img`, comes in as a flat 784 vector.

Another way to prevent an autoencoder from simply copying the input to the output is the addition of *noise*. Here we use "noise" in the technical sense of random events that corrupt the original image, which in this context would be called the *signal*. In a *de-noising autoencoder* we add noise to the image in the form of randomly zeroed pixels. Typically about 50% of the pixels might be degraded in this way. The AE loss function is again the squared-error loss, this time between the pixels in the uncorrupted image and the output decoder image.

7.2   Convolutional Autoencoding

The last section built up an AE for Mnist digits using an encoder to reduce the initial image of 784 pixels first to 256 and then to 128. Having done this,

$$
\begin{array}{cccc}
1 & 2 & 3 & 4 \\
4 & 3 & 2 & 1 \\
2 & 1 & 4 & 3 \\
3 & 4 & 1 & 2
\end{array}
\quad\rightarrow\quad
\begin{array}{cccccccc}
0 & 0 & 0 & 0 & 0 & 0 & 0 & 0 \\
0 & 1 & 0 & 2 & 0 & 3 & 0 & 4 \\
0 & 0 & 0 & 0 & 0 & 0 & 0 & 0 \\
0 & 4 & 0 & 3 & 0 & 2 & 0 & 1 \\
0 & 0 & 0 & 0 & 0 & 0 & 0 & 0 \\
0 & 2 & 0 & 1 & 0 & 4 & 0 & 3 \\
0 & 0 & 0 & 0 & 0 & 0 & 0 & 0 \\
0 & 3 & 0 & 4 & 0 & 1 & 0 & 2
\end{array}
$$

Figure 7.3: Padding an image for decoding in a convolutional AE

the decoder reversed the process, in the sense that starting with 128 "pixels", we build the image first back to 256, and then 784. All this was done with fully connected layers. The first had a weight matrix of shape [784, 256], the second [256, 128], and then, for the decoder, [128, 256] followed by [256, 784]. However, as we learned from our earlier exploration of deep learning in computer vision, best results come from the use of convolution. In this section we build an AE using convolutional methods.

The convolutional encoder to reduce image dimensions is unproblematic. In Chapter 3 we noted how, say, horizontal and vertical strides of two reduce the image size by a factor of two in each dimension. In Chapter 3 we were not concerned with compressing the image, so counting in the channel size (how many filters we applied to each image patch), we actually ended up with more numbers describing the image at the end of the convolution process than at the start (the 7 by 7 image times 32 different filters gives 1568). Here we definitely want the encoded intermediate layer to have many fewer values than the original image, so we might, say do three layers of convolution, the first layer taking us to $14 * 14 * 10$, the second to $7 * 7 * 10$, and the third $4 * 4 * 10$ (the exact numbers, are, of course, hyperparameters).

Decoding with convolution is much less obvious. Convolution never increases image size, so it is not obvious how upsampling might work. The solution is quite literally to expand the input image before we convolve it with a bank of filters. In Figure 7.3 we consider the case where the hidden layer of the AE is a $4 * 4$ image and we want to expand it to an $8 * 8$ image. We do so by surrounding each "real" pixel with enough zeros to create an $8 * 8$. (The real pixel values are for illustration only.) This requires adding to each real pixel value zeros to the left, diagonal left, and up. As you might expect, by adding enough zeros we can expand the image to whatever size we want. Then, if we convolve this new image with conv2d, a stride of one, and Same padding, we end up with a new $8 * 8$ image.

```
mnist = input_data.read_data_sets("MNIST_data")

orgI = tf.placeholder(tf.float32, shape=[None, 784])
I = tf.reshape(orgI, [-1,28,28,1])
smallI = tf.nn.max_pool(I,[1,2,2,1],[1,2,2,1],"SAME")
smallerI = tf.nn.max_pool(smallI,[1,2,2,1],[1,2,2,1],"SAME")
feat = tf.Variable(tf.random_normal([2,2,1,1],stddev=.1))
recon = tf.nn.conv2d_transpose(smallerI, feat,[100,14,14,1],
                                            [1,2,2,1],"SAME")
loss = tf.reduce_sum(tf.square(recon-smallI))
trainop = tf.train.AdamOptimizer(.0003).minimize(loss)

sess = tf.Session()
sess.run(tf.global_variables_initializer())

for i in range(8001):
    batch = mnist.train.next_batch(100)
    fd={orgI:batch[0]}
    oo,ls,ii,_ =sess.run([smallI,loss,recon,trainop],fd)
```

Figure 7.4: Transpose convolution on a Mnist digit

So we get an appropriately sized image, but does it have appropriate values? To see how it might Figure 7.4 gives TF code to illustrate upsampling with convolution. There we first downsample an Mnist image and then upsample using convolution. The downsample is done in two steps:

```
smallI=tf.nn.max_pool(I,[1,2,2,1],[1,2,2,1],"SAME")
smallerI=tf.nn.max_pool(smallI,[1,2,2,1],[1,2,2,1],"SAME")
```

The first command creates a $14 * 14$ version of the image with each original separate $2 * 2$ patch represented by the highest pixel value in that patch. See the left-hand image in Figure 7.5 for an example of a $14 * 14$ image of a "7." The second command creates a still smaller $7 * 7$ version. The next two lines of Figure 7.4 (`feat`, `recon`) create `recon`, an upsampled reconstruction of the $7 * 7$ image back to $14 * 14$, as illustrated in the right-hand image of Figure 7.5. Figure 7.4 does not illustrate how we normally use convolutional upsampling, which is meant to follow convolutional downsampling. Rather we wanted to start with an understandable image, so we could better see what happened to it. From Figure 7.5 we see that while the reconstruction is hardly perfect, it basically worked. (We replaced zeros by blanks in the figure to make the 7's outline clearer.)

```
                                        6  6  2  2  5  5  6  6
      9  9        4  5  9  9            5  6  2  2  5  5  5  6
   9  9  9  9  9  9  9  9      6  6  6  6  6  6  6  6  6  6
   9  9  9  9  9  9  9  7      5  6  5  6  5  6  5  6  5  6
   8  8           9  9  9      5  5  5  5  6  6  6  6
                  9  9  5      5  5  5  5  5  6  5  6
            6  9  9                  6  6  6  6
            8  9  9                  5  6  5  6
            9  9  7            1  1  6  6  4  4
      1  9  9  1               1  1  5  6  4  4
      4  9  9                  2  2  6  6
      1  9  4                  2  2  5  6
```

Figure 7.5: 14 ∗ 14 Minst 7, and version reconstructed from 7 ∗ 7 version

The key line in Figure 7.4 is the call to `conv2d_transpose`. As we just mentioned, the common case is the use of `conv2d_transpose` to "undo" a use of standard `conv2d`, as in:

```
tf.nn.conv2d(img,feat,[1,2,2,1],"SAME")
```

This call would downsample the image that the `conv2d_transpose` can upsample. If we ignore the third argument to the transpose version, the arguments to the two functions are exactly the same. However they do not all have the same import. Yes, in both cases the first argument is the 4D tensor to manipulate, and the second is the bank of convolutional filters to use. But `conv2d_transpose`, no matter what the stride and padding arguments say, is going to use stride one and Same padding. The purpose of these arguments is rather to determine how to add all the extra zeros, as in Figure 7.3 — e.g., to undo the contraction due to a stride of two we would generally want to pad every real pixel with three extra zero pixels, as in Figure 7.3.

Unfortunately, it is not possible completely to determine the output image size of `conv2d_transpose` just from this information. Thus the third argument to `conv2d_transpose` is the size of the desired output image. In Figure 7.4 this is [100, 14, 14, 1]: 100 is the batch size, we want a 14 ∗ 14 output image, and only one channel. The situation that causes the ambiguity comes from strides greater than one with Same padding. For example, consider two images, one 7 ∗ 7 and one 8 ∗ 8. In both cases, if we convolve with a stride of two and Same padding, we end up with an image of size 4. Thus, going the other way, `conv2d_transpose` with stride two and

0	0	0	0	1	−1	1	−1	1	−1
0	0	0	0	−1	0	−1	0	−1	0
0	−1	1	−1	1	−1	0	−1	0	0
−1	0	−1	0	−1	0	−1	0	0	0
0	0	1	−1	1	−1	1	−1	0	−1
0	0	−1	0	−1	0	−1	0	−1	0
0	−1	0	−1	0	0	1	−1	1	−1
−1	0	−1	0	0	0	−1	0	−1	0
1	−1	1	−1	1	−1	1	−1	0	0
−1	0	−1	0	−1	0	−1	0	0	0
0	0	0	0	0	0	0	0	0	0
0	0	0	0	0	0	0	0	0	0

Figure 7.6: Upsampled small Mnist digit from zeroth training example

Same padding cannot know which of these output images the user intends.

To this point in talking about transpose convolution we have concentrated on making sure to pad the input in such a way as to get the desired upsampling effect. We have not concerned ourselves with how the filters manage this task. Indeed, at the start of training they do not. Figure 7.6 shows the upsampled image at the zeroth training example. The predominant visible effect in the figure is the alternations of 0 and −1, which is no doubt an artifact arising from the alternation of zero padding values and nonzero real pixel values in the image fed into conv2d_transpose. There is a mathematical theory of how transpose convolution can find the correct kernel values, but for our purposes we only need to know that variable kernel values and back propagation do it for us.

As for using conv2d_transpose for autoencoding, it is exactly analogous to fully connected autoencoding. We have one or more layers of downsampling using conv2d, possibly using max_pool or avg_pool, followed by typically an equal number of upsampling layers using conv2d_transpose.

7.3   Variational Autoencoding

A *variational autoencoder* (we say *VAE* for short) is a variant of AEs in which the goal is not to reproduce exactly the image we started with, but rather to create a new image that is a member of the same class of images but recognizably new. It gets its name from *variational methods*, a topic in Bayesian machine learning. Again, we fall back on our friendly Mnist data set. Our initial goal for our VAE is to input an Mnist digit image and get

```
            0  0  0  0  0  0  0
            0  0  1  0  0  0  0
            0  0  1  0  0  0  0
            0  0  1  0  0  0  0
            0  0  1  0  0  0  0
            0  0  1  0  0  0  0
            0  0  0  0  0  0  0


   0  0  0  0  0  0  0          0  0  0  0  0  0  0
   0  0  0  0  1  0  0          0  0  1  0  0  0  0
   0  0  0  0  1  0  0          0  0  0  0  0  0  0
   0  0  0  0  1  0  0          0  0  0  0  0  0  0
   0  0  0  0  1  0  0          0  0  1  0  0  0  0
   0  0  0  0  1  0  0          0  0  1  0  0  0  0
   0  0  0  0  0  0  0          0  0  0  0  0  0  0
```

Figure 7.7: An original image and two "reconstructions"

out a new image that is both recognizably similar and different.

If we do not care that the new one is recognizably different, then standard autoencoding would pretty much solve the problem. After all, look again at Figure 7.2, our AE reconstruction of the '7' from the beginning of the book (Figure 1.1). At the time we were proud of how similar they are, but of course they are not identical. However, they are so close that had we printed this later version in gray scale it would very hard to distinguish from Figure 1.2. Furthermore, some thought should indicate that a standard AE with squared-error loss is not really what we want. Consider the three $7 * 7$ images in Figure 7.7. The top is intended to be a small image of a 1, and the other two are supposed to be reconstructions of the first. The first of these looks similar to the original, but because the digit is shifted over by two pixels there are no overlapping values, and its mean squared error when compared to the top image in Figure 7.7 is 10. Furthermore, the bottom right image is actually more similar according to our loss function as it only differs in two pixels. So standard autoencoding and squared error loss are not really suitable for our task. However, put this objection to the side for the moment in order to concentrate on how VAE works. We come back to this issue later and show how VAEs solve the problem.

Looking a little way under the hood, our program is going to input an image and then conjure up a vector of random numbers, and it is these random numbers that control the difference between the original and the new images — put in the same image/random-numbers pair and we get the exactly the same variant of the input image. Later we see that we can omit the image, in which case we get out not a variation on a particular image, but rather a completely new image in the overall style of all the images. This will typically look like one of the possible digits, but depending on how well the VAE is doing its job it might not. If you skip ahead to Figure 7.10 you can see some examples.

A diagram of the VAE architecture is shown in Figure 7.8. An image comes in at the bottom of the diagram and we can trace the computation up through the encoder. The encoded information is then used to create not a single image embedding, but rather two vectors of reals, σ and μ. We then construct a new image embedding by generating a vector of random numbers $\mathbf{r}$, and computing $\mu + \sigma \mathbf{r}$. Here μ can be thought of as the original embedded version of the image, and we perturb it with $\sigma \mathbf{r}$ to get a different embedding which is near, but not too near, the original. This revised embedding then goes though a standard decoder to produce a new image. If we are using the program (as opposed to training it) this new image is output to the user. If we are training, the new image is fed into the "image loss" layer. The image loss is just the squared loss of the difference in pixel values between the original and new images. So the source of output image variation in a VAE is $\mathbf{r}$. If we input the same image and the same vector of random numbers, we get the same image out.

To say this again in slightly different words, μ is the basic encoded version of the input image, just as always this chapter, while σ specifies the legal bounds on how much we can vary the input image and still have it a "recognizable" version. Remember, both σ and μ are real-number vectors of size, say, 10. If $\mu[0] = 1.12$ it means that the encoded image should have as its first real a number more or less close to 1.12, with the variation around 1.12 controlled by $\sigma[0]$. If $\sigma[0]$ is large (and our NN is working properly) it means that it is possible to vary the first dimension of the encoded image quite a bit without making the output version unrecognizable. If $\sigma[0]$ is small, then it is not.

But there is a big problem here. We have assumed that somehow the σs and μs we get from the encoder will be numbers such that $\mu + \mathbf{r} * \sigma$ is a reasonable image encoding. If the loss is just the squared-error loss we do *not* get the result we want.

This is where VAEs veer into deep math, but we are going to ask the reader instead to accept some semi-plausible changes to our loss function. VAEs have two losses that are added together to give the total loss. One we have already seen, the squared-error loss between the original image pixels

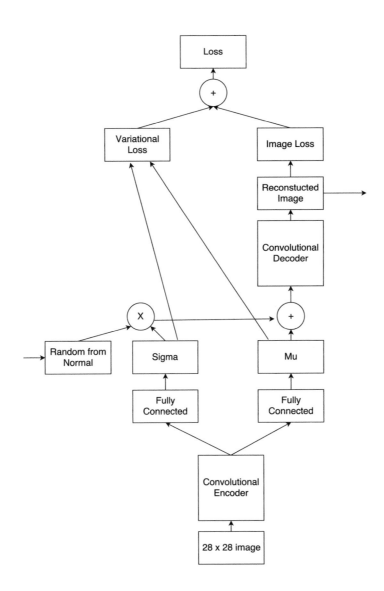

Figure 7.8: Structural model of a variational autoencoder

and those of the reconstruction. We call this the *image loss*.

The second of the losses is the *variational loss*:

$$L_v(\mu, \sigma) = -\sum_i \frac{1}{2}(1 + 2\sigma[i] - \mu[i]^2 - e^{2\sigma[i]}) \qquad (7.4)$$

This is for an single example, and it is a pointwise computation over σ and μ. (Remember, they are both vectors.) To make this more comprehensible, consider what happens if we set first σ then μ to zero:

$$L_v(\mu, 0) = \mu^2 \qquad (7.5)$$

$$L_v(0, \sigma) = -\frac{1}{2} - \sigma + \frac{e^{2\sigma}}{2} \qquad (7.6)$$

From the first of these equations we see that the NN is being pushed to keep the mean values $\mu = 0$. Of course the image loss is going to counteract this push quite a bit, but everything else equal, L_v wants $\mu \approx 0$.

The second of the above equations is going to keep σ sort of near 1. When σ is less than 1 the second term of $L_v(0, \sigma)$ dominates and we decrease the loss by increasing σ, whereas when σ is larger than 1 the third term begins to get large quite fast.

That this looks like a standard normal distribution is not a coincidence. If we had gone through the math we would have understood (a) why it is a good idea to encourage the image encoding to look more like a standard normal and (b) why the minimal variation loss is not exactly at $\sigma = 1$. Instead, we ask the reader to accept that adding this second loss function to our overall calculation give us what we want: an NN that, given a multidimensional σ and μ computed by our NNs on the basis of a real Mnist image, produces the encoding of a new, slightly different image I' from:

$$I' = \mu + \mathbf{r}\sigma \qquad (7.7)$$

where $\mathbf{r}$ is a vector of random numbers themselves produced from a standard normal distribution. Once we have this assurance, we have our VAE.

Let us return to the issue we raised earlier (page 145) to the effect that a standard AE with squared loss does not really fit the goal we set for VAEs: to produce noticeably different versions of an image that are, at the same time, noticeably similar. Our example of the problem in Figure 7.7 was two imaginary reconstructions of a 1, one translated two pixels horizontally, one missing two pixels in the middle of the vertical stroke. According to squared-error loss the second was more similar, but the first would be a good

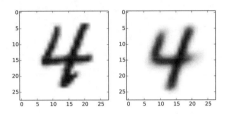

Figure 7.9: An original image and a VAE reconstruction

VAE reconstruction while the second would not. The claim is that, working properly, VAEs overcome this difficulty.

First, note that yes, when training VAEs we do use squared-error loss, but by their very nature VAEs have to accept a larger squared loss because they can only reconstruct the original image up to some deliberately engineered randomness. Next note that this randomness is situated in the image encoding in the middle of the VAE architecture. The claim is that this is the best place for it if VAEs are to work properly.

Mostly implicit but sometimes explicit in our discussion of AEs is the observation that they achieve dimensionality reduction by noting commonalities between inputs. They tailor embedding to assume the common features, only "mentioning" the differences. Suppose, as is reasonable, Mnist digits differ slightly in their position on the page. Then one way to exploit this fact to make the encoding small is to have, say, one of the real numbers in the encoding specify the overall horizontal position of the digit. (Or perhaps, with only twenty reals in which to encode the mean for a number 1, we cannot afford to devote a real to this job, and our AE "decides" some other variation is more important for a good reconstruction of our image. This is only an illustration.) The point is, if there is a real that encodes the overall horizontal position, then the lower-left image of Figure 7.7 is, in fact, very close to the upper original — it differs only at one encoding position.

At any rate, VAEs do work. Figure 7.9 shows an original Mnist 4 and a new version. Even a few seconds' study is sufficient to convince you that they are different. Furthermore, they are different in a way quite typical for VAEs (or at least for less than great VAEs)— the right image, the reconstruction,

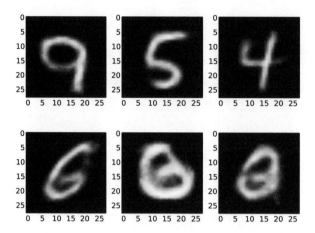

Figure 7.10: VAE Mnist digits generated from scratch

is less distinctive. It is a blander 4, if you will. Most noticeably, the left-hand 4 (the original) has an uptick on the bottom of the major vertical stroke that is completely missing on the right.

So far we have considered the problem of generating an image that is similar to, but recognizably different from, an input image. However, we earlier noted that VAEs can also work more freely — given a general class of images, produce another member of that class. This is a much harder problem to do well, but the VAE hardly changes at all. Training, in fact, is exactly the same. The only difference is how we use the VAE. To produce a new image not based upon an existing one, the VAE generates a random number (again from a standard normal) but this time inserts it (via **feed_dict**) to be used as the entire image encoding. Figure 7.10 shows some examples of the results from the same program that generated the examples in Figure 7.9, but this time no image was given to emulate. Four of the images are recognizably Mnist-like digits, but the bottom-right image seems to be a "3-8" and the one just before it is a mighty poor excuse for an 8. A stronger model, a lot more training epochs, and more attention to hyperparameters would produce a much better result.

Before leaving VAEs, a few words for those who would like to better understand the variational loss of Equation 7.4. In our original formulation, we generate a new image I' upon an original I. To do this we use a convolutional encoder C to produce a reduced representation $z = C(I)$. Here we concentrate on two probability distributions, $\Pr(z \mid I)$ and $\Pr(z)$. In particular, we first assume that both are normal distributions.

If you just passed placidly from the last sentence to this one, you are either not thinking too hard about what I am saying or you are much smarter than I. How can we simply assume that a distribution for something as complicated as real-world images, or even MNIST digits, is as simple as a normal distribution? Admittedly, this will be an n-dimensional normal, where n is the dimension of the image representation produced by the convolutional encoder C, but even n-dimensional normals are pretty simple things — a 2D normal is bell shaped.

The key idea to keep in mind is that $\Pr(z)$ is a probability distribution based not on the original image, but on the representation $C(I)$. You may remember that earlier we might have an element of the representation capture how far the center of a digit was away from the center of the image, so that the digit '1' at the top of Figure 7.7 has a representation very similar to the bottom-right version. Suppose we are able to carry this program to its logical end so that every parameter in the representation vector is a number like this, some specification of the fundamental ways one image of a number can differ from another. Other examples might be "major downstroke location" or "diameter of topmost circle" (for 8s), etc. As you might imagine the diameter of the top circle in an 8 might typically be, say, 12 pixels, but it could be significantly higher or lower. In such a case it would make a lot of sense to describe the variation in this parameter as a normal with mean 12 and standard deviation, say, 3. As for $\Pr(z \mid I)$, being normal, similar reasoning applies. Given an image, we want the VAE to produce many different similar but different images. The probability of any one of them could reasonably be a normal distribution on key factors such as diameters of circles in 8s.

There are still many steps before we get to the variational loss of Equation 7.4, but we are just going to take one or two of them. We further assume that $\Pr(z)$ is a standard normal — a normal distribution with $\mu = 0$ and $\sigma = 1$ — written $N(0, 1)$. On the other hand, we assume that the output of the encoder is a normal distribution whose mean and standard deviation are dependent on the image itself, e.g., $N(\mu(I), \sigma(I))$. This explains (a) why we have the encoder of Figure 7.8 lead to two values labeled μ and σ, and (b) why, in order to get random variation, we picked numbers according to a standard normal.

We take one last step. The assumptions that one of the normals is standard and the other not cannot be in general satisfied. Rather we just try to minimize the discrepancy. We can model a particular image more closely if we are free to pick appropriate μs and σs and we are pushed in this direction by the image loss. On the other hand, we want those values to be as otherwise close to 0 and 1 as possible, and this is where the variational loss comes in.

To put this another way, we want to minimize the difference between two probability distributions $N(0, 1)$ and $N(\mu(I), \sigma(I))$. A standard measure of the difference between two distributions is the *Kullback-Leibler divergence*:

$$D_{KL}(P \parallel Q) = \sum_i P(i) \log \frac{P(i)}{Q(i)} \qquad (7.8)$$

For example, if $P(i) = Q(i)$ for all i then the ratio of the two is always 1, and $\log 1 = 0$. So we can now characterize the goal of a VAE as minimizing image loss while simultaneously minimizing $D_{KL}(N(\mu(I), \sigma(I)) \parallel N(0, 1))$. Fortunately there is a closed-form solution to minimizing the latter, and with some more algebra (and a clever idea or two) this leads to the variational loss function presented above.

7.4   Generative Adversarial Networks

Generative adversarial networks, or *GANs* for short, are unsupervised NN models that work by setting two NN models in competition with each other. In the Mnist setting the first network (called the *generator*) would generate a Mnist digit from scratch. The second, the *discriminator*, is given the output of the generator or an example of a real Mnist digit. Its output is its estimate of the probability that the input it was given is from the real example, not the one generated by the generator. The discriminator's decision then acts as the error signal to both models but in "opposite directions," in the sense that if it is certain of a correct decision that means a large error to the generator (for not fooling this discriminator), while if the discriminator is badly fooled, that is a large loss for the discriminator.

As with AEs in general, a GAN can be used for learning the structure of the input data without labels. Also, as with VAEs in particular, GANs can generate new variants of a class, prototypically a class of images but in principle almost anything. GANs are a hot topic in deep learning because in some sense they are a *universal loss function*. Any set of pictures, text, planning decisions, etc., for which we have data can be used for unsupervised GAN learning with the same basic loss.

The basic architecture of a GAN is shown in Figure 7.11. To understand how it works, we take a trivial example: the discriminator is given two

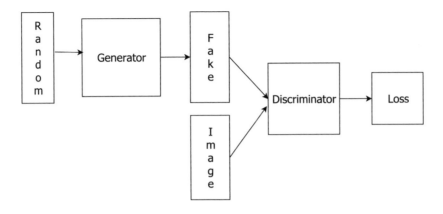

Figure 7.11: The structure of a generative adversarial network

numbers, one at a time. One, the "real" data, is generated by a normal distribution with, e.g., mean 5 and standard deviation 1, so the numbers it produces are mostly between 3 and 7. The "fake" number is generated by the generator, which is a one-layer NN. (For this section only the opposite of a "real" number is a fake number, not a complex one.) The generator is given a random number, equally likely to be anywhere between –8 and +8. In order to fool the discriminator it must learn to modify the random number, presumably to make it come out between 3 and 7. Initially the generator NN has parameters close to zero, so, in fact, it mostly produces numbers close to zero as its output.

GANs exercise several aspects of TF we have not covered so far, and we give the complete code for the simple GAN in Figure 7.12. We have numbered each small section of the code for reference.

First, look at section 7 where we train the GAN. Pick out the main training loop, which we have set for 5001 iterations. The first thing we do is to generate some real data — a random number near 5 — and a random number between –8 and 8 to feed the generator. We then update, separately, first the discriminator then the generator. Finally, every 500 iterations we print out tracking data.

We come back to this code section in a bit, but first we consider at a high level how things should work. We want the discriminator to output a single number (*o*) that is intended to be the probability that the number it has just seen is from the real distribution. Look briefly at section 3 of the code. When we execute the function `discriminator` it sets up a four-layer fully connected feed-forward NN. The first three layers have `relu`

```
bSz, hSz, numStps, logEvery, genRange = 8, 4, 5000, 500, 8

1 def log(x): return tf.log(tf.maximum(x, 1e-5))

2 with tf.variable_scope('GEN'):
    gIn = tf.placeholder(tf.float32, shape=(bSz, 1))
    g0=layers.fully_connected(gIn, hSz, tf.nn.softplus)
    G=layers.fully_connected(g0,1,None)
gParams =tf.trainable_variables()

3 def discriminator(input):
    h0 = layers.fully_connected(input, hSz*2,tf.nn.relu)
    h1=layers.fully_connected(h0,hSz*2, tf.nn.relu)
    h2=layers.fully_connected(h1,hSz*2, tf.nn.relu)
    h3=layers.fully_connected(h2,1, tf.sigmoid)
    return h3

4 dIn = tf.placeholder(tf.float32, shape=(bSz, 1))
with tf.variable_scope('DIS'):
    D1 = discriminator(dIn)
with tf.variable_scope('DIS', reuse=True):
    D2 = discriminator(G)
dParams = [v for v in tf.trainable_variables()
                if v.name.startswith('DIS')]

5 gLoss=tf.reduce_mean(-log(D2))
dLoss=0.5*tf.reduce_mean(-log(D1) -log(1-D2))
gTrain=tf.train.AdamOptimizer(.001).minimize(gLoss, var_list=gParams)
dTrain=tf.train.AdamOptimizer(.001).minimize(dLoss, var_list=dParams)

6 sess = tf.Session()
sess.run(tf.global_variables_initializer())

7 gmus,gstds=[],[]
for i in range(numStps+1):
    real=np.random.normal(5, 0.5, (bSz,1))
    fakeRnd= np.random.uniform(-genRange,genRange,(bSz,1))
    #update discriminator
    lossd,gout,_ = sess.run([dLoss,G,dTrain],{gIn:fakeRnd, dIn:real})
    gmus.append(np.mean(gout))
    gstds.append(np.std(gout))
    # update generator
    fakeRnd= np.random.uniform(-genRange,genRange,(bSz,1))
    lossg, _ = sess.run([gLoss, gTrain], {gIn:fakeRnd})
    if i % logEvery == 0:
        frm=np.max(i-5,0)
        cmu=np.mean(gmus[frm:(i+1)])
        cstd=np.mean(gstds[frm:(i+1)])
        print('{}:\t{:.3f}\t{:.3f}\t{:.3f}\t{:.3f}'.
            format(i, lossd, lossg, cmu, cstd))
```

Figure 7.12: GAN for learning mean of a normal distribution

activation functions, and the last uses a sigmoid. Since sigmoids output numbers between 0 and 1, as we noted earlier they are good for producing numbers intended to be probabilities (the probability that the input is from the real distribution). More specifically, the output is interpreted as the probability that the input is a member of a class (the class of real inputs). This determines our choice of loss function — we use cross-entropy loss.

When the discriminator is fed a number from the real normal, distribution (n_r), the loss is the negative log of the discriminator NN output (o_r). When the discriminator is fed the generated fake number the loss is $\ln 1 - o_f$. Be sure to see, in Figure 7.12 section 7, that in the training loop we first create some real numbers, then some random numbers to give to the generator. Just after the comment "update discriminator" we do just that by giving the Adam optimizer both. The discriminator loss function L_d is given by:

$$L_d = \frac{1}{2}(-\ln(o_r) - \ln(1 - o_f)) \qquad (7.9)$$

If you look at section 5, where we lay out the loss and training code, you see the discriminator loss defined as in Equation 7.9. Here o_r is the the degree to which the discriminator believes the real input is indeed real. Conversely, the loss also includes a term that penalizes the discriminator to the degree it believes the fake (generated) number (o_f) is real.

So consider what might happen on the first training example. As we already noted, the generator outputs something close to zero, say 0.01. The real sample from our normal distribution might be 3.8. However, the discriminator's parameters are also initialized near zero so o_r and o_f are both near zero. Initially L_d is going to be dominated by the $-ln(o_r)$ term, which goes negative infinity as o_r goes to zero, but the program quickly learns not to assign any probabilities too close to zero.

More important is how the derivative of the loss affects the discriminator's parameters. Looking back at the single-layer network of Chapter 1, we see that the derivative of the weight parameters is proportional to the input for the weight in question (Equation 1.22). If we go through the math we find that when we give the discriminator the real sample the weight moves upward proportionally to the sample value (e.g., 3.8). Conversely, the same weight is moved downward when we train on the fake generator value, but that is only 0.01, so the discriminator is moving slightly toward saying that higher input values are the real ones.

Next we look at how the program should grade the performance of the generator. Well, the generator wants to fool the discriminator in the sense that when the latter is fed the output of the former, the generator wants the discriminator to think that it has just seen the real, not fake, numbers. So the the generator loss L_g should be:

$$L_g = -ln(o_f) \tag{7.10}$$

The reader should verify that the first line of section 5 of the GAN code defines the generator loss exactly this way.

So to summarize what we have said so far: section 7, the main training loop, first trains the discriminator by giving some real and some fake numbers with a loss function that penalizes mistakes in both directions, real judged as fake, and vice versa. Then it trains the generator with loss based just on how well the discriminator correctly identifies the generator's fakes.

Unfortunately, things are a bit more complicated. First, note that section 4 has two calls to the code to set up a discriminator. The reason is that in TF you cannot feed a single network separately from two different sources (as opposed to say, feeding a network with the concatenation of two tensors). So we create, in some sense, two discriminators. One, D1, is fed from the real distribution, whereas the second receives as its input the fake from the generator D2.

Of course, we do not really want two separate networks, so to unify them we insist that the two networks share the same parameters, thus computing exactly the same function and not taking up much more space than a single version. This is the purpose of the calls to `tf.variable_scope` we see in section 4. We first made use of this TF function in Chapter 5 (see page 99). There we needed two LSTM models and we needed to avoid naming conflicts, so we defined one within a variable scope "enc" (encoder) and one within "dec" (decoder). Within the first of these all the variables defined would have "enc" prepended to their names, and in the second, "dec." Here we have the opposite concern. We want to avoid having two separate sets, so we give both scopes the same names, and on the second call we explicitly tell TF to reuse the same variables by adding `reuse = True`.

There is one last complication to deal with before moving on. Section 7 of Figure 7.12 shows us first training the discriminator, then the generator, at each training step. Furthermore, to train the discriminator we feed TF two random numbers, the real sample and a random number to feed to the generator. We then run the generator to create a fake number, and the probability that the discriminator assigns to this number as coming from the true distribution o_f. The latter is part of the loss defined in Equation 7.9. However, in the absence of any special handling, on the backward pass the generator parameters are also modified, and worse, are modified in a way to make the discriminator's loss smaller. As noted above, this is *not* what we want. We want the generator's parameters to move so as to make the discriminator's task more difficult. Thus, when we run back propagation and change discriminator parameters in section 5 (see the line that sets `dTrain`), we instruct TF only to change one of the two sets of parameters. In particular, note the named argument to `AdamOptimizer`. This argument tells the optimizer (on this particular call) to modify only the TF variables in the list.

As for how the classes of parameters, `gParams` and `dParams`, are defined, consult the ends of sections 2 and 4. The TF function `trainable_variables` returns a tensor of all the variables in the TF graph defined up to that point.

7.5 References and Further Readings

The origins of autoencoding in NNs may be lost in the mists of time. The textbook by Goodfellow et al. [GBC16] cites Yann LeCun's PhD thesis [LeC87] as its earliest reference on the subject.

Of the topics mentioned in this chapter, the first that seems to have achieved a distinct identity within the NN community is variational autoencoders. The standard reference here is a paper by Diederik Kingma and Max Welling [KW13]. I found the blog by Felix Mohr [Moh17] very useful, and my code is based upon his. If you have the statistical prerequisites and would like to get at the math behind VAEs, I found Carl Doersch's VAE tutorial a good reference [Doe16].

The history of GANs, however, is completely clear that the basic idea emerged in pretty much its current form in a paper by Ian Goodfellow et al. [GPAM+14]. I learned a lot from John Glover's blog [Glo16]. My code for the GAN for learning a normal distribution is based upon his, and he in turn credits [Jan16].

The comment that GANs are "universal" loss functions (page 152) is from a talk by Phillip Isola [Iso] that presents many interesting ways to achieve unsupervised learning of visual processing, with particular emphasis on using GANs.

7.6 Written Exercises

Exercise 7.1: Consider downsampling with fully connected layers. Mnist digits always have rows of zeros around the edges. Given our comment to the effect that AEs work by having the image encoding ignore commonalities, what does this imply (all else equal) about the values of the trained first-level weights?

Exercise 7.2: Same situation and question as in Exercise 7.1, but now about the trained weights for the last layer before the output.

Exercise 7.3: Give a call to `conv2d_transpose` that performs the transposition shown in Figure 7.3.

Exercise 7.4: Assuming that `img` is a $2*2$ pixel array of the numbers 1 to 4, show the padded version of the following call to `conv2d_transpose`:

```
tf.nn.conv2d_transpose(img,flts,[1,6,6,1],[1,3,3,1],"SAME")
```

You may ignore the first and last components of the shape.

Exercise 7.5: This is not important, but why did we set the GAN training loop to 5001 iterations in Figure 7.12 rather than 5000?

Exercise 7.6: The GAN of Figure 7.12 prints out both an average mean of the generated data, which we used to judge the accuracy of the GAN, and the standard deviation of the generated data, which we ignored above. In point of fact, despite the fact that we set the real numbers' standard deviation to 0.5 (point out where this is done!), the actual σ printed out after each 500 iterations started out higher, quickly decreased below 0.5, and seems to be headed lower still. Explain why this GAN model has no pressure on it to learn the correct σ, and why it is reasonable that the actual value it comes up with is lower than the real one.

Appendix A

Answers to Selected Exercises

A.1 Chapter 1

Exercise 1.1. If a is the digit value of the first training example, then after training on that one example only the value b_a should increase, and for all digit values $a' \neq a$, $b_{a'}$ should decrease.

Exercise 1.2, (a) The forward-pass logits are $.(0 * .2) + (1 * -.1) = -.1$ and $(0 * -.3) + (1 * .4 * 1) = .4$, respectively. To compute the probabilities we first compute the softmax denominator $e^{-.1} + e^{.4} = .90 + 1.50 = 2.40$. Then the probabilities are $.9/2.4 = .38$ and $1.5/2.4 = .62$. (b) The loss is $-\ln .62 = -1.9$. From Equation 1.22 we see that $\Delta(0,0)$ is going to be a product of terms involving $x_0 = 0$, so $\Delta(0,0) = 0$.

Exercise 1.5. Computing the matrix multiplication gives us

$$\begin{pmatrix} 4 & 7 \\ 8 & 15 \end{pmatrix}. \tag{A.1}$$

Then, adding the right-hand side vector to both rows, we get:

$$\begin{pmatrix} 8 & 12 \\ 12 & 19 \end{pmatrix} \tag{A.2}$$

Exercise 1.6. The derivative of the quadratic loss with respect to b_j is computed almost exactly as we showed for cross-entropy loss except

$$\frac{\partial L}{\partial l_j} = \frac{\partial}{\partial l_j}(l_j - t_j)^2 = 2(l_j - t_j) \tag{A.3}$$

Since the derivative of l_j as a function of b_j is 1, it follows that

$$\frac{\partial L}{\partial b_j} = 2(l_j - t_j) \tag{A.4}$$

A.2   Chapter 2

Exercise 2.1. If we do not specify a reduction index it is assumed to be zero, in which case we add columns. This gives us [0, 3.2, 9].

Exercise 2.2 This new version is significantly slower than the original since on every iteration of the main training loop it creates a new gradient-descent optimizer rather than using the same one each time.

Exercise 2.4. You cannot take the tensordot because the dimensions are not equal. If you could, the first tensor argument has shape [4, 3], and the second [2, 4, 4]. If you just concatenate them you get [4, 3, 2, 4, 4]. Since we are taking the dot product of the 0th component of the first tensor and the 1st component of the second, they drop out, giving [3, 2, 4], the shape of the result.

A.3   Chapter 3

Exercise 3.1. (a) One example would be

```
-2   1   1
-2   1   1
-2   1   1
```

As for part (b), the point is there are infinitely many such kernels. Multiplying the numbers in the above kernel by any positive number will be an example.

Exercise 3.5. In terms of syntax the only difference is the stride of [1, 1, 1, 1] rather than the earlier [1, 2, 2, 1]. Thus we apply maxpool on every $2 * 2$ patch, rather than on every other one. When the stride of maxpool is 1, the shape of `convOut` is same as the input iimage, whereas with stride 2 it is approximately half the size in both height and width. Thus the answer to the first question is "no." It is also not the case that they have the same set of values since, e.g., if we had two patches of small values right next to each other but surrounded by larger values, the single-pixel-stride output would include the larger of these two small values, while in the double-pixel-stride these values would be "drowned out" by the neighboring pixel values. Lastly, the third answer is "yes" in that every pool value in the first case is repeated in the second case, but not vice versa.

Exercise 3.6a Each kernel we create has shape [2, 2, 3], which implies 12 variables per kernel. Since we create 10 of them, 120 variables are created. Since the number of times we apply a kernel has nothing to do with its size/shape, neither the batch size (100) nor height/width (8/8) have any effect on this answer.

A.4   Chapter 4

Exercise 4.2. The important difference between seting $\mathbf{E}$ to 0 (or to all ones) is that the NN never sees the actual input, but only its embedding. Thus setting all the embeddings to the same value has the effect of making all words identical. Obviously this defeats any chance of learning anything.

Exercise 4.3 Actually computing the total loss when using L2 regularization requires computing the sum of weight squares for all the weights in the model. This quantity is not needed elsewhere in the computation graph. For example, to compute the derivative of the total loss with respect to $w_{i,j}$ only requires adding $w_{i,j}$ to the regular loss.

Exercise 4.5. First, yes, it can do better than picking from a uniform distribution. It should learn to assign higher probability to more common words (e.g., "the"). Note, however, that a unigram model has no "input" and thus no need for embeddings or linear unit input weights. It does, however, need biases, as it is by modifying these that it learns to assign probabilities according to word frequency.

A.5   Chapter 5

Exercise 5.2 The more complicated attention mechanism uses the decoder state after time t to decide on the attention used in decoding at time $t + 1$. But obviously we do not know this value until we have processed time t. In back propagation through time we process a window of words all at the same time. Except for the very first position in the decoder window, we do not have the incoming state value we need for the computation. In essence, then, we need to write a new back-propagation-through-time mechanism.

Exercise 5.4 (a) We want good machine translation. To the degree that the other loss function affects things, it is presumably in moving the weights so they perform less well at this task. Thus performance is degraded. (b) But part (a) is true only for the training data. It says nothing about performance on the other examples. Adding the second loss function should help the program learn more about the structure of French. This should improve its performance on new examples, which are the bulk of the test data.

A.6   Chapter 6

Exercise 6.3. In value iteration the only way a state can get a nonzero value is if either (a) there is a way to get an immediate reward by an action from that state (only state 14), or (b) one can take an action from that state that leads to a state that already has a nonzero value (states 10, 13, and 14). So all other states must retain their zero values. State 10 has a maximum Q value for $Q(14, l)$, $Q(14, d)$, and $Q(14, r)$. In each case the values are from ending up in state 15, and are $.33 \cdot .9 \cdot .33 = .1$, so $V(10) = .1$. In exactly the same way, $V(14) = .1$. Lastly, $V(15)$ gets its value from $Q(15, d)$ or $Q(15, r)$. In both cases the computation is $.33 \cdot .9 \cdot .1 + .33 \cdot .9 \cdot .33 + .33 * 1 = .03 + .1 + .33 = .47$.

Exercise 6.4. We stated that if, when we computed possible actions in REINFORCE, we had saved their probabilities we would be able to compute the loss on the second pass without starting from a state and then computing the probabilities. However, if we did this and did NOT redo the computation leading from the state to the action probabilities, then TF's backward pass would not be able to trace the computation back through the fully connected layers that compute the actions from the state. Thus that layer (or layers) would not have its values updated and the program would not learn to compute better action recommendations for states.

A.7   Chapter 7

Exercise 7.1. To ignore the value of the border, the obvious thing to do is to set the values that connect the pixels to the first layer to zero. Let x be pixel values in the 1D version of the image $0 < x < 783$. If i, j range over pixels in the $28 * 28$ image, then for all x such that $x = j + 28i$, $i < 2$ or $i > 25$, and $j < 2$ or $j > 25$, for all $y, 0 \le y \le 256$:

$$\mathbf{E_1}(x, y) = 0$$

Exercise 7.3.

```
tf.nn.conv2d_transpose(smallerI,feat,[1,8,8,1],[1,2,2,1],"SAME")
```

Exercise 7,5 We wanted the tracking values to print out after the last iteration. If we had set the range to 5000 the last iteration would have been 4999 and not printed.

Bibliography

[BCB14]   Dzmitry Bahdanau, Kyunghyun Cho, and Yoshua Bengio. Neural machine translation by jointly learning to align and translate. *arXiv preprint arXiv:1409.0473*, 2014.

[BCP⁺88]   Peter Brown, John Cocke, S Della Pietra, V Della Pietra, Frederick Jelinek, Robert Mercer, and Paul Roossin. A statistical approach to language translation. In *Proceedings of the 12th conference on computational linguistics*, pages 71–76. Association for Computational Linguistics, 1988.

[BDVJ03]   Yoshua Bengio, Réjean Ducharme, Pascal Vincent, and Christian Jauvin. A neural probabilistic language model. *Journal of machine learning research*, 3(Feb):1137–1155, 2003.

[Col15]   Chris Colah. Understanding LSTM networks. http://colah .github.io/posts/2015-08-Understanding-LSTMs/, August 2015.

[Doe16]   Carl Doersch. Tutorial on variational autoencoders. *ArXiv e-prints*, August 2016.

[GB10]   Xavier Glorot and Yoshua Bengio. Understanding the difficulty of training deep feedforward neural networks. In *Proceedings of the thirteenth international conference on artificial intelligence and statistics*, pages 249–256, 2010.

[GBC16]   Ian Goodfellow, Yoshua Bengio, and Aaron Courville. *Deep learning*. MIT Press, 2016.

[Gér17]   Aurélien Géron. *Hands-on machine learning with Scikit-Learn and TensorFlow: concepts, tools, and techniques to build intelligent systems*. O'Reilly Media, 2017.

[Glo16]   John Glover.   An introduction to generative adversarial
             networks (with code in tensorflow).   http://blog.aylien.com
             /introduction-generative-adversarial-networks-code-
             tensorflow/, 2016.

[GPAM+14] Ian Goodfellow, Jean Pouget-Abadie, Mehdi Mirza, Bing
             Xu, David Warde-Farley, Sherjil Ozair, Aaron Courville, and
             Yoshua Bengio. Generative adversarial nets. In *Advances in
             neural information processing systems*, pages 2672–2680, 2014.

[HS97]   Sepp Hochreiter and Jürgen Schmidhuber. Long short-term
             memory. *Neural computation*, 9(8):1735–1780, 1997.

[Iso]   Phillip Isola. Learning to see without a teacher. https://www
             .youtube.com/watch?v=ck3_7tVuCRs.

[Jan16]   Eric Jang. Generative adversarial nets in tensorflow (part i).
             http://blog.evjang.com/2016/06/generative-adversarial-nets
             -in.html, 2016.

[Jul16a]   Arthur Juliani. Simple reinforcement learning with tensor-
             flow part 0: Q-learning with tables and neural networks.
             https://medium.com/emergent-future, 2016.

[Jul16b]   Arthur Juliani. Simple reinforcement learning with tensorflow
             part 2: Policy-based agents. https://medium.com/emergent-
             future, 2016.

[KB13]   Nal Kalchbrenner and Phil Blunsom. Recurrent continuous
             translation models. In *EMNLP*, volume 3, page 413, 2013.

[KH09]   Alex Krizhevsky and Geoffrey Hinton. Learning multiple layers
             of features from tiny images. *Technical report, University of
             Toronto*, 2009.

[KLM96]   Leslie Pack Kaelbling, Michael L Littman, and Andrew W
             Moore. Reinforcement learning: a survey. *Journal of artifi-
             cial intelligence research*, 4:237–285, 1996.

[Kri09]   Alex Krizhevsky.   The CIFAR-10 dataset.   https://www.cs
             .toronto.edu/]=-kriz/cifar.html, 2009.

[KSH12]   Alex Krizhevsky, Ilya Sutskever, and Geoffrey E Hinton. Im-
             agenet classification with deep convolutional neural networks.

In *Advances in neural information processing systems*, pages 1097–1105, 2012.

[Kur15]   Andrey Kurenkov. A 'brief' history of neural nets and deep learning, parts 1–4. http://www.andreykurenkov.com /writing/, 2015.

[KW13]   Diederik P Kingma and Max Welling. Auto-encoding variational Bayes. *arXiv preprint arXiv:1312.6114*, 2013.

[LBBH98]   Yann LeCun, Léon Bottou, Yoshua Bengio, and Patrick Haffner. Gradient-based learning applied to document recognition. *Proceedings of the IEEE*, 86(11):2278–2324, 1998.

[LBD+90]   Yann LeCun, Bernhard E Boser, John S Denker, Donnie Henderson, Richard E Howard, Wayne E Hubbard, and Lawrence D Jackel. Handwritten digit recognition with a backpropagation network. In *Advances in neural information processing systems*, pages 396–404, 1990.

[LeC87]   Yann LeCun. *Modèles connexionnistes de l'apprentissage (connectionist learning models)*. PhD thesis, University of Paris, 1987.

[MBM+16]   Volodymyr Mnih, Adria Puigdomenech Badia, Mehdi Mirza, Alex Graves, Timothy Lillicrap, Tim Harley, David Silver, and Koray Kavukcuoglu. Asynchronous methods for deep reinforcement learning. In *International conference on machine learning*, pages 1928–1937, 2016.

[Mil15]   Steven Miller. Mind: how to build a neural network (part one). https://stevenmiller888.github.io/mind-how-to-build-a-neural-network, 2015.

[Moh17]   Felix Mohr. Teaching a variational autoencoder (VAE) to draw Mnist characters. https://towardsdatascience.com /@felixmohr, 2017.

[MP43]   Warren S McCulloch and Walter Pitts. A logical calculus of the ideas immanent in nervous activity. *Bulletin of mathematical biophysics*, 5(4):115–133, 1943.

[MSC+13]   Tomas Mikolov, Ilya Sutskever, Kai Chen, Greg S Corrado, and Jeff Dean. Distributed representations of words and phrases and their compositionality. In *Advances in neural information processing systems*, pages 3111–3119, 2013.

[Ram17]   Suriyadeepan Ram. Scientia est potentia. http://suriya deepan.github.io/2016-12-31-practical-seq2seq/, December 2017.

[RHW86]   David E Rumelhart, Geoffrey E Hinton, and Ronald J Williams. Learning representations by back-propagating errors. *Nature*, 323(6088):533, 1986.

[RMG+87]   David E Rumelhart, James L McClelland, PDP Research Group, et al. *Parallel distributed processing*, volume 1,2. MIT Press, 1987.

[Ros58]   Frank Rosenblatt. The perceptron: A probabilistic model for information storage and organization in the brain. *Psychological review*, 65(6):386, 1958.

[Rud16]   Sebastian Ruder. On word embeddings — part 1. http:// ruder.io/word-embeddings-1/index.html#fnref:1, 2016.

[SB98]   Richard S Sutton and Andrew G Barto. *Reinforcement learning: An introduction*, volume 1. MIT Press, 1998.

[Ten17a]   Google Tensorflow. Convolutional neural networks. https:// www.tensorflow.org/tutorials/deep_cnn, 2017.

[Ten17b]   Google Tensorflow. A guide to TF layers: Building a neural network. https://www.tensorflow.org/tutorials/layers, 2017.

[TL]   Rui Zhao Thang Luong, Eugene Brevdo. Neural machine translation (seq2seq) tutorial. https://www.tensorflow.org /tutorials/seq2seq.

[Var17]   Amey Varangaonkar. Top 10 deep learning frameworks. https://datahub.packtpub.com/deep-learning/top-10-deep -learning-frameworks/, May 2017.

[Wil92]   Ronald J Williams. Simple statistical gradient-following algorithms for connectionist reinforcement learning. *Machine learning*, 8(3-4):229–256, 1992.

Index